commercial art techniques

LEON AMIEL · PUBLISHER

NEW YORK

A PRACTICAL SELF-INSTRUCTION COURSE
AND REFERENCE HANDBOOK
OF METHODS AND PROCEDURES
OVER 500 ILLUSTRATIONS

commercial art techniques

Revised Edition

S. Ralph Maurello

Television Art Director
State University College of Arts and Science
Plattsburgh, New York

Author of "The Complete Airbrush Book"
"Paste-ups and Mechanicals"

Dedicated to the Memory of
My Mother and Father

ACKNOWLEDGEMENTS

My thanks and deep appreciation to the following persons
not otherwise credited in this book: Peninah Neimark, whose
astute editing and advice lessened the burden of this revised
edition; Manuel Weinstein, the publisher's Production Manager
when this book was first published, and who served in the same
capacity for other books by the author during the past twenty-two
years; Roy Jensen, Production Manager for this new edition; my wife,
Beki, who helped prepare the mechanical for this book; and
Nick Strychalski, artist-friend of long standing, who helped me
re-penetrate the fortress of New York City, which I left some
time ago for the quiet beauty of the Adirondacks.

DESIGN AND LAYOUT BY THE AUTHOR
MANUFACTURED IN THE UNITED STATES OF AMERICA

ISBN: 0-8148-0612-0
LCC 74-29153

Contents

COMMERCIAL ART

**advertising
· promotion**

**publishing
· communications**

**business
· industry**

**education
· instruction**

decoration

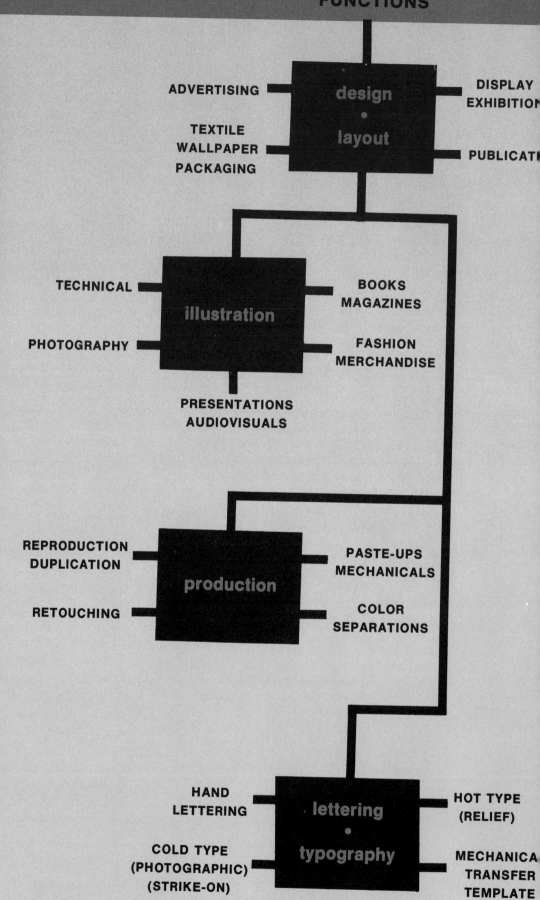

ADVERTISING

**design
·
layout**

DISPLAY
EXHIBITION

TEXTILE
WALLPAPER
PACKAGING

PUBLICATION

TECHNICAL

illustration

BOOKS
MAGAZINES

PHOTOGRAPHY

FASHION
MERCHANDISE

PRESENTATIONS
AUDIOVISUALS

REPRODUCTION
DUPLICATION

production

PASTE-UPS
MECHANICALS

RETOUCHING

COLOR
SEPARATIONS

HAND
LETTERING

**lettering
·
typography**

HOT TYPE
(RELIEF)

COLD TYPE
(PHOTOGRAPHIC)
(STRIKE-ON)

MECHANICAL
TRANSFER
TEMPLATE

Introduction

Literally defined, commercial art consists of those forms of art which are prepared for and serve the needs of business, education, advertising and related fields. It might, however, be more meaningful to define commercial art in terms of the specific functions it performs, and also to differentiate it, insofar as possible, from the so-called "fine arts."

Before the advent of halftone printing and photography, the commercial artist was thought of primarily as an illustrator, at first for books, newspapers and magazines, and then increasingly for advertising. Now, however, there are many more areas of application of commercial art which fit into the broad categories of communication graphics and the decorative arts. The former category is exemplified by television, books, periodicals, film projections, etc.; the latter by textile print design, gift wrappings, wallpaper, etc.

The basic functions which the commercial artist performs are *design, illustration, lettering, typography,* and *production procedures.* Depending upon the versatility of the artist, the project involved, and the job requirements, all these functions might be performed by one artist, or, as is more often the case, by several artists, each specializing in a particular aspect. The applications and functions of commercial art might be better understood if viewed in chart form (see opposite page).

While there is no sole criterion for differentiation between the commercial arts and the fine arts, several combined factors are more representative of commercial art: the commercial artist works on assignment from a specific client and does a specific job within a stated time, for a definite application and for a specified fee. On the other hand, the fine artist, theoretically at least, usually does whatever artwork he or she desires, initiates the project himself, does it in whatever manner he wishes, takes whatever time he feels necessary and generally does not have a specific buyer for the project when it is completed, or perhaps ever. In addition, one of the most important aspects of commercial art is that it is almost always prepared for *reproduction* in some other form, such as a printed poster, a newspaper illustration or a color slide, whereas in the fine arts, the *original* work of art itself is the most important form, any subsequent reproduction or duplication of the artwork generally being incidental to the original. However, these criteria do not hold for all cases, as may well be exemplified by the fact that the portrait artist, who is considered a fine artist, works on assignment for a specific client and for a predetermined fee. Conversely, a display or exhibition unit, definitely a commercial art project, might very well consist of original art and lettering viewed directly by the public, rather than in printed or other reproduced form. I do not wish to belabor the comparison, because personally I do not think the distinction important except in terms of vocational choice, certain aspects of training and the fact that the commercial artist has more restrictions and requirements that have to be adhered to. There are highly creative and competent artists in both the fine and commercial arts, just as there are uninspired hacks in both areas. More than ever before, the so-called commercial artist faces a challenging, innovative and intellectually demanding field with ever expanding horizons.

This book has several objectives: to provide an overview of the commercial art profession in terms of functions and applications; to provide specific information on methods and procedures related to graphic arts functions; to serve as a handbook for instructors, students and professional artists; to serve as an aid to those who, though not artists themselves, utilize artwork or the services of artists—such people as educational communications specialists, TV art directors, technical manual writers, editors, advertising personnel, etc.

S. Ralph Maurello
Elizabethtown, New York

1. Commercial Art Functions

THE FUNCTIONS performed in commercial art may be classified into four major divisions: 1. Illustration, 2. Lettering/Typography, 3. Design and Layout, 4. Production Procedures. While there are overlapping functions and characteristics in each of these divisions, detailed considerations in the following chapters will help to clarify them.

Illustration

Illustration (*Fig. 1.1*) is the graphic representation or interpretation of a scene, incident, idea, process, object or person, actual or imaginary. It may serve to visualize a story, a magazine cover, a calendar, an advertisement, a cartoon, a map, technical material, an architectural or product design, television material, film animation, visual aid, merchandise drawing, fashion drawing, etc. The extensiveness of this function of commercial art is obvious.

Fig. 1.2: Varityper Subsidiary, Addressograph Multigraph Corporation.

Lettering and Typography

The uses and forms of lettering and type (*Fig. 1.2*), as well as the methods of producing these forms, are very important to the commercial artist involved in visual communication by means of words and pictures—communications graphics. Specific letter and type forms must be selected, appropriate sizes of type determined, and space and arrangement on the page or other visual medium have to be decided upon and indicated. (Although the latter is actually a design and layout function, it is usually handled by the person who selects the type, at least in the preliminary stage.) Not only mechanical, but considerable creative abilities are required for these procedures. The methods involved are numerous and often quite complicated, requiring manual and procedural skills. This is an area of specialization, as well as of general application. Considering the quantity and diversity of such materials, the scope and importance of lettering and typography are apparent.

Fig. 1.1: Walter Skor © 1974. Reprinted with permission from *The Saturday Evening Post*. The Curtis Publishing Company.

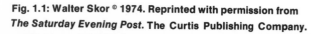

Fig. 1.3: Paper Makers Advertising Association.

Design and Layout

The term "design," as applied to commercial art, might be considered the creative aspect of graphics, whether the graphics serve a communications purpose (*Fig. 1.3*), as would an advertisement, or a decorative purpose, as would art conceived for a textile print. Layout is the arrangement and form given to various units of illustrative material and reading matter on a flat surface such as a printed page; it is design, or planning and visualization, as applied to individual advertisements, entire publications, visual aids, etc.

In designing a book, for example, the designer would establish the size of the pages, kind of paper, typefaces, size and arrangement, and perhaps even the form and size of illustrations (photos or drawings). However, another artist would probably do the actual illustrations, still another any hand lettering involved, and another the mechanical preparation of this material for printing. A design for a textile print, on the other hand, might well be *entirely* conceived and executed by the designer. The term "design" refers both to the functions involved as well as the physical artwork or finished product.

Production

Most material prepared for printing and other forms of reproduction or transmission, such as slide projection or television, consists of *verbal* information, in the form of lettering or type, and *illustrative* information, in the form of art or photography. Each of these may consist of many different units, and the finished material may have been executed by various artists, photographers or specialists. All of these units have to be planned, prepared, assembled and coordinated (*Fig. 1.4*) so that they can be properly utilized in the final product, whether that be a printed page, a billboard, a television commercial or an instructional color slide; therefore a knowledge of the mechanics of the print media and nonprint media involved is essential. Operations such as pasting the units in position, making overlays for color plates, retouching, etc. fall into the category of production functions. A knowledge of these functions is important to the commercial artist, whether he be an illustrator, designer, layout artist or art director because it enables him to properly plan and execute the artwork and also to achieve graphic effects not obtainable directly in the artwork itself. To some extent these skills can be learned in a classroom or from books or other forms of instruction, but skill and judgment can only be acquired by performing these functions and seeing their results in the finished reproduction or medium utilized.

Fig. 1.4: S.R.Maurello, State University of New York, Plattsburgh.

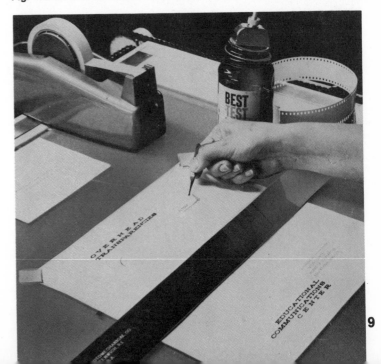

9

2. Media and Techniques of Illustration

SINCE THE ARTIST'S LANGUAGE, whether verbal or pictorial, is a visual one, anything he wishes to communicate must be in some graphic form. The artist works with line, tone and color to graphically present his ideas. There are many materials, tools and methods used to prepare visual messages. Those most generally used in illustration are presented in this chapter.

One of the problems confronting the beginner and often the professional in commercial art is that of deciding what medium and technique to use. The problem may be related only to a particular assignment, or it may be a question of deciding what to adopt for permanent use. The term "medium" as used here refers to the material with which the artist works, such as pencil, pen and ink, tempera, etc. These are briefly charted on the next three pages for quick comparison and handy reference. ("Medium" can also refer to the vehicle of communication, such as TV, etc.)

Techniques

"Technique" refers to the *method of handling* the medium or materials to achieve the desired effects. Good technique is generally acquired only after much practice and use of a specific medium. Although techniques in any medium may vary to such an extent with different artists that their work is thereby identifiable, certain basic procedures and characteristics exist. After control of the materials and procedures is acquired, the artist can adapt them to his own form of expression.

The beginner usually advertises his uncertainty by the use of conflicting techniques in the same illustration; his work is not consistent in quality, and it appears to have been done by two or three different persons. After more experience he is likely to eliminate methods which are foreign to his own temperament, natural ability or to the subject matter, and he will have developed a working technique through which he can express visually what he wishes to convey. What he does with it will determine whether he is a creative artist or merely a technician.

Media

In this section are discussed all the media commonly used by the commercial artist for all types of illustration. On the next few pages, a small example of each medium or technique is shown with a brief description, followed by a portion of finished illustration done in that medium. Further on in the book, each particular technique will be discussed and illustrated in greater detail. In each instance the various tools and materials are pictured or discussed; working procedures are shown in step-by-step illustrations; and characteristics of the medium and examples, diverse in both style and application, are reproduced.

The art media have been arranged in two distinct groups, according to the manner in which the art is reproduced. These general classifications are: *line* media—those which consist only of solid black (or any solid color) and white values; and *continuous tone* media—those made up of black, white and intermediate values of gray. *Color* media may be either line media or continuous tone media or both. Though many of these may appear the same in printed form, the materials used and working methods are different, as well as is cost of reproduction. The selection of the art medium depends upon the manner in which the artwork is to be used or reproduced, the personal choice of the artist, and the subject matter or type of art being done.

Continuous Tone Media

PENCIL

More refined than the ordinary writing pencils, graphite drawing pencils are available in many degrees of softness and hardness, and in various shapes and sizes. Carbon, charcoal and chalk pencils and sticks can be used also in the same manner.

Fig. 2.1: Gustav Rehberger

OPAQUE WATERCOLOR

Poster colors, gouache, designer colors, tempera and retouch grays are known as opaque watercolors because they are opaque and thick compared with the fluid transparency of transparent watercolors. Opaque watercolors can also be used semi-transparently. (Acrylic paints fall into this category.

Fig. 2.2: Howard Koslow.

TRANSPARENT WATERCOLOR

"Watercolor" generally denotes the transparent, as opposed to the opaque, pigment or dye color medium, and the artwork is known as a watercolor painting. Illustrations done with water-diluted India ink, lampblack or ivory black are known as wash drawings.

Fig. 2.3: Bob Herrmann , Lord & Taylor.

AIRBRUSH

A small, delicate version of the familiar spray gun, the airbrush is used with dyes and watercolors, both transparent and opaque. Airpainting gives soft, smoothly blended tones and colors.

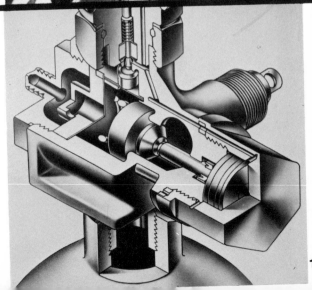

Fig. 2.4: S.R. Maurello, Walter Kidde & Co.

PASTEL

Pastel is dried pigment and a binder pressed into stick form and made in soft and hard grades. It is a very "direct" medium, capable of subtle tonal and color qualities, but not fine detail. Though permanent, it is easily smeared.

Fig. 2.5: Milton Herder.

Line Media

PEN, BRUSH AND INK

India ink, colored inks and dyes are used with a drawing pen or ruling pen on paper or board. Many types of pens can be used, including felt, ballpoint, nylon tip, etc., as well as brushes.

Fig. 2.6: Reese Brandt.

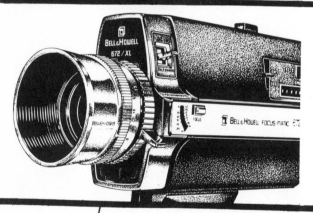

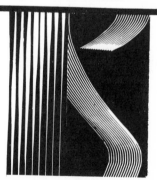

SCRATCHBOARD

A scratchboard is a white, chalk coated board to which ink is applied with brush or pen. White lines or areas can be scratched or scraped from the inked areas with extreme fineness and precision. Freehand and "loose" techniques can be used.

Fig. 2.7: Courtesy of Bell & Howell Co.

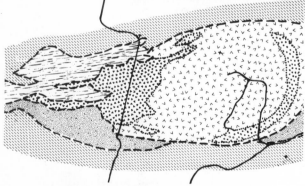

REARING POND INTRUSION   ADJACENT UNITS
Gabbro
Eucrite
Peridotite
Granite
Anorthositic &
Ferro-gabbro
Volcanics

SHADED LINE MEDIA

When pencil or crayon is applied to a paper board with an embossed pattern, varied shading effects from light gray to black will be obtained, depending upon the pressure or amount of coverage. The drawing can be reproduced as line copy. Transparent acetate sheets with printed black and white shades and patterns can be applied to drawings.

Fig. 2.8: James F. Olmsted.

Other Media

COLOR AIDS

Colored papers, colored acetate sheets, colored and patterned tapes are often used to partially, and sometimes completely, execute illustrations, diagrams, maps and visual aids.

Fig. 2.9: S.R.Maurello, State University of New York,

PHOTOGRAPHY

Photography is a widely used medium which the commercial artist, art director and layout artist should know thoroughly. Aside from the use of "straight" photographs, many variations of the photographic process result in effects that are particularly useful in the advertising, editorial, instructional and illustrative fields.

Fig. 2.10: Appleton Coated Papers.

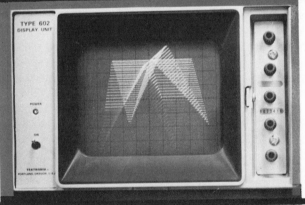

COMPUTER ART

The computer can execute drawings and solve design problems that are programmed by artist, engineer or designer. Drawings are made by several methods: with stylus pen on paper; electronically on a cathode ray tube; or by type machine.

Fig. 2.11: Tektronix.

SPECIAL EFFECTS

Many effects obtained in reproduction are not the result of any specific medium, but may be the result of special art, photography or reproduction methods, or a combination of these. Shown here is a paper sculpture, in itself a three-dimensional art form, but in this case used as a graphics application.

Fig. 2.12: Old Colony Envelope Company.

Fig. 2.13: Larry Johnson, Wolper Productions, Inc.

Fig. 2.14: *University Review*, State University of New York.

Fig. 2.15: Courtesy of Bell & Howell Co.

Style

"Style" is the interpretative visual form the artist gives to his subject matter. We might consider it an abstract quality as compared with the physical quality of "technique." Some artists interpret subject matter very realistically; they attempt to graphically represent things as they actually appear, whereas other artists prefer a more "interpretive" or personal visualization— a decorative, "stylized" or impressionistic treatment. Compare the literal handling of the figure at right (*Fig. 2.15*), with the modified treatment given the one directly below it and the abstract handling of others on the next page. Here are distinct differences in style, the result of the artists' interpretations rather than the medium, the technique or the subject, which is basicaly that of the human form.

Artists may be selected for assignments on the basis of their style, as well as the quality of their work, not only for illustration but also for layout and design (*Fig. 2.13*). Some artists work with a free, loose technique and others employ a tight, precise treatment; some are very conservative, and others are more inventive and imaginative. Whatever the style, it is the artist who governs it, not the medium—witness such diverse results obtained in each of the media in the following chapters.

Fig. 2.16: E. McKnight-Kauffer.

Fig. 2.17: Herb Lubalin, Art Director, Sudler & Hennessey. On this page are exemplified various treatments of the same subject by different artists working in the same studio. Although the identical source—the top left illustration—subject matter and format were used, note how diverse are the results, even in the same medium. The differences are due to the diverse "styles" of the individual artists.

3. Pencil

THE PENCIL is not ordinarily thought of as a medium for finished art-work. However, it is useful both for roughing in ideas and for finished art. In addition to lead or graphite pencils, carbon, chalk and colored pencils can be used to advantage in commercial art-work.

Types of Pencils and Their Uses

Lead and graphite pencil marks have a slight sheen, whereas carbon and chalk have a matte finish and give a richer black than graphite (*Fig. 3.4*). Graphite and lead are used in various forms—round lead pencils, flat lead pencils, and square and round graphite sticks which can be used in the hand or in mechanical holders. Graphite pencils are graded according to softness (B grades) and hardness (H grades). The softer grades give correspondingly darker images—from 2B, 3B, etc. up to 6B, which is the softest and darkest. HB is medium. H, 2H, etc. are progressively harder and lighter in tone, up to 7H. Thus, by selecting the lead of the proper density as well as varying the pressure used on the pencil, the artist is able to control tones. The size of the stroke and the textural effects obtainable are governed by the type and size pencil used, the manner in which it is sharpened, the manner in which it is held and the surface on which it is used. This is illustrated on the next two pages.

Wolff, Conte, carbon and chalk pencils also come in various degrees of softness. All give an appearance of blackness when used on a paper with a slight tooth or texture, as compared with the grayish effect of the lead pencil.

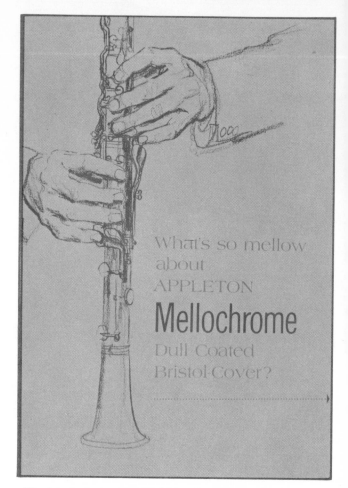

Pencil can be used on any kind of paper stock, though a shiny paper does not take hard lead very well. A rough paper will naturally take the pencil only on the higher ridges, resulting in a granular effect (*Fig. 3.5*). Where necessary, this can be altered by rubbing down the penciled area with a paper stump or with the finger; this gives almost the effect of a wash (*Fig. 3.6*). One can now work over this with the same or a softer pencil, giving a darker effect. Highlights can be obtained with a kneaded eraser (*Fig. 3.7*).

Grease pencils and AV pencils in black and color are useful for marking on acetate, glass and other glossy surfaces.

Sharpening a pencil for drawing is best done by carefully shaving off the wood with a razor blade, then shaping the lead to the desired form on a sandpaper pad as shown (*Fig. 3.2*). Either a sharp point, a chisel edge, a round, oval or square-shaped lead can be secured in this manner (see page 18). Sandpaper pads are sold in art supply stores.

Fig. 3.2: Shaping Pencil Point on Sandpaper Pad.

In *Fig. 3.3*, at the right, a square graphite stick is being used to make a fairly wide stroke. Other effects can be obtained by handling it in the same manner as the pastel stick illustrated on page 45. A mechanical holder can be used for graphite or crayon sticks.

Fig. 3.3

Fig. 3.4: Different Types of Pencils.

| 4H LEAD | HB LEAD | 4B LEAD | LAYOUT PENCIL | CARBON PENCIL | FLAT LEAD | GRAPHITE STICK | LEAD HOLDER |

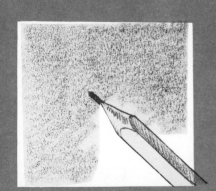

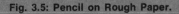

Fig. 3.5: Pencil on Rough Paper.   Fig. 3.6: Smudging Pencil with Paper Stump.   Fig. 3.7: Picking Out Highlights

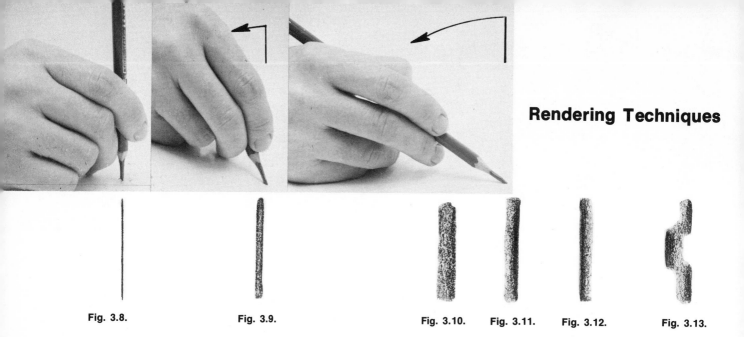

Fig. 3.8.   Fig. 3.9.   Fig. 3.10.   Fig. 3.11.   Fig. 3.12.   Fig. 3.13.

When the lead being shaped on the sand-paper pad is held at a constant angle and rubbed back and forth, an oval-shaped point will result. If the pencil is now held vertically, as in *Fig. 3.8*, a sharp thin line can be drawn with the edge of the lead, moving in the direction of the arrow or opposite direction. A broad stroke of consistent width, as shown in *Fig. 3.9*, can be drawn with the same lead by making the stroke with the oval point held flat on the paper, as was done when sandpapering the point. If the point is sharpened while held at a lower angle on the sandpaper, the same diameter lead will give a much broader stroke (*Fig. 3.10*). If the stroke is made with the heel of the point slightly raised from the paper it will result in a stroke with a sharp edge on one side and a soft edge where the surface of the point is slightly raised from the paper (*Fig. 3.11*). By raising the toe of the point a soft edge can be obtained on the opposite side of the stroke (*Fig. 3.12*). By alternating the pressure so that the heel is raised for part of the stroke and the toe for another part, a soft edge can be changed from one side to the other in the same stroke (*Fig. 3.13*).

Chisel-edged, round, and square-tipped leads will give the variations shown in *Fig. 3.14*. These various shaped leads can be used to advantage in lettering as well as sketching. In layout lettering the varied strokes can be used to indicate Roman type letters as compared with Gothic, and for drawing serifs, etc. In each instance in *Fig. 3.14* the pencil was held at the same angle for the horizontal as well as the vertical stroke. Stroke direction is indicated by the arrows. A chisel-edged lead, the end view of which is shown below the pencil (*Fig. 3.14A*), will give a thin line on the horizontal stroke and a line as thick as the width of the lead itself on the vertical stroke. A round lead sharpened to an oval point, as in *Fig. 3.10*, and held flat against the paper, will give a broad line on the horizontal (*Fig. 3.14B*). A round lead held vertically to the pad will give lines of the same width in both horizontal and vertical strokes (*Fig. 3.14C*). The ends of the strokes will be circular as shown. The pencil itself should be held vertically when making such strokes. A square leaded pencil will give the same width line in the horizontal and vertical strokes but will have square ends (*Fig. 3.14D*) as compared to the round ones in *Fig. 3.14C*.

Fig. 3.14: **Various Shaped Leads and Their Effects.**

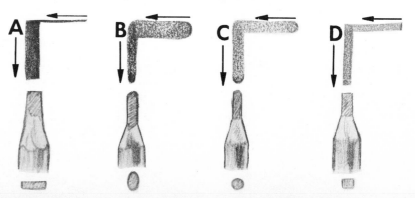

Fig. 3.15:
Joseph Hirsch, *The Lamp*.

Fig. 3.17:
David Stone Martin,

Fig. 3.18: James Crabb, *Ford Times*.

Fig. 3.19: From "51 House Plans," by Rudolph A. Mattern.

A diversity of both techniques and styles are represented in these examples of pencil drawings. Note the characteristic tone and line effects in the drawings, handled somewhat differently in each, according to the artist's style.

Fig. 3.20: Melbourne Brindle, Matson Lines.

Melbourne Brindle's drawing, above, is an excellent example of the Wolff pencil medium. Note the extreme range of values, from the strong blacks to the light gray tones of the sand and buildings. This reproduction was made from a proof of an advertisement, yet it does not suffer much loss of quality. The very dark areas were done with soft pencils, the lighter areas and details with hard pencils. Mr. Brindle planned his drawing and values carefully. An illustration board with only a very slight tooth is best for this medium, as even this will give a definite granular texture. Areas requiring an overall, smooth gray tone can be rubbed down with a paper stump, as was shown for the graphite.

Carbon or graphite pencil can be used in combination with wash. The illustration at left employs this combination. First the pencil drawing is made, then a flat wash applied, and finally the pencil strokes strengthened where they have been dulled by the wash overlay.

Fig. 3.21: Courtesy of Eastman Kodak Co.

Fig. 4.1A: Howard Koslow.

4. Opaque Watercolor

OPAQUE WATERCOLORS are used for illustration, but are particularly applicable to design and mechanical illustration because they can be controlled more easily than the transparent colors, although the latter blend more readily. Watercolors designated as "tempera," "designers colors" and "gouache" are the best grade of opaque colors and are available under numerous brand names, as are "poster colors."

Opaque watercolor is a heavier and stiffer medium than transparent watercolor. An opaque color, laid over any other color, whether light or dark, covers and replaces it. By contrast, a truly transparent color is effective only when placed over a color of the *same* or *lighter* value. With opaques, you can start at any value and work up to lighter or down to darker values (*Fig. 4.1*), whereas with transparent color you cannot lighten the color of an area. It is possible, of course, to combine the two techniques; that is, to start with a dark transparent color and work up the light areas or details with opaques. This method is used effectively in illustration.

Opaque watercolors are obtainable in all colors, plus black, white and various premixed shades of gray (*Fig. 4.3*). While black and white paint can be mixed by the user to make any value, it is not only more convenient to procure the premixed grays, but it is more practical because any gray can thus be matched by merely using it from the corresponding tube or jar. The different colors are also made up in value scales so that different values of any color can be readily used and controlled. The premixed grays, usually called "Retouch Grays," are made by several different manufacturers.

Acrylics can be used in the same manner as opaque watercolor, but become insoluble when dry. Acrylics are best used with nylon brushes.

Fig. 4.1B: Jeremiah Goodman
Lord & Taylor.

Fig. 4.2A: Lamp Black.

Fig. 4.2B: Opaque White.

Fig. 4.3: Retouch Grays.

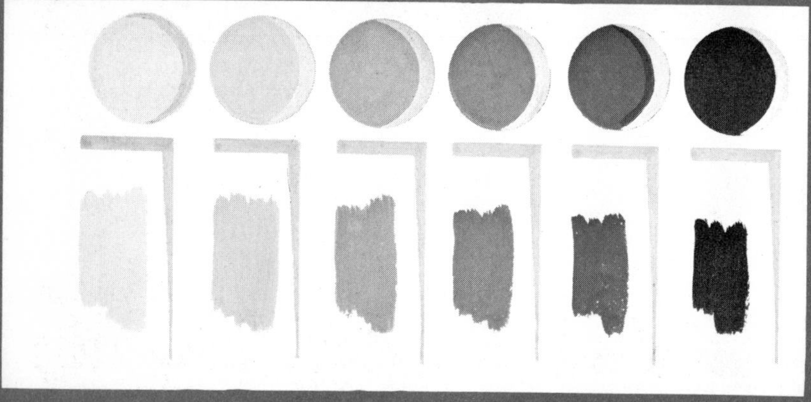

Fig. 4.4: Porcelain Palette.

Fig. 4.5: Flat Bristle Brush.

Fig. 4.6: Red Sable Brush.

Fig. 4.7: Paper Stocks.

COLORED PAPER

ILLUSTRATION BOARD

WATERCOLOR PAPER

Equipment and Materials

When working with the scaled grays, place them in the palette in consecutive order, as shown in *Fig. 4.4*. The type of palette illustrated holds the colors in the round wells, with the flat wells serving for mixing or thinning. The black and white are best kept in separate single porcelain dishes so that they will not be contaminated. When through working for the day, place a few drops of water in each well, and the colors will remain soft for future work.

Either red sable or bristle brushes may be used; the former (*Fig. 4.6*) for smooth, fine work, the latter (*Fig. 4.5*) for coarser, thicker painting. Opaque paints can be used on colored paper, illustration board, watercolor paper (*Fig. 4.7*) and drawing paper. Except when used in an airbrush, they should not be applied to slick paper unless a "streaky" effect is desired. They handle very well on gesso panels.

Techniques

Achieving a flat area of uniform value with opaques presents no problem because the color can be taken directly from the tube or mixed to the proper shade. The pigment is slightly diluted with water to about the consistency of heavy cream and applied to the paper smoothly with the brush (*Fig. 4.8A*). Do not load the brush too heavily with color. Proceed uniformly over the area in one direction with each stroke slightly overlapping the preceding one, but without leaving a ridge of paint. You can work back into the painted area while the color is still wet, to smooth it out. If necessary, the whole area can be covered again with the same or another color after the previous one has dried.

The opacity of the colors is shown in *Fig. 4.8B*, where a white, a light gray, a dark gray and a black have been painted over the light gray tone.

BLENDING. The transition from one value to another may be achieved in several different ways. A good poster and design technique, in which the art restrictions call for flat tones only (that is, no actual blending of colors) is shown in *Fig. 4.9*. The light and dark colors are placed side by side in *Fig. 4.9A*, and in *Fig. 4.9B* the transition is made with a narrow band of color halfway in value between the two colors to be joined. This can be carried further, as in *Fig. 4.9C*, where several values are used to make the transition. When mixing colors for such an effect start with the two extremes, L and D (light and dark); mix these together to make the middle value, M; mix M and L to get the middle light value, ML; mix M and D to get the middle dark value, MD, and so on in both directions.

In a wet blend, *Fig. 4.10*, one color is brushed on, as in *Fig. 4.10A*, then the next color is immediately applied with a slight overlap, which allows the colors to blend along the edge as in *Fig. 4.10B*. It is also possible to soften the sharp edge, after the colors have dried, by wetting it slightly with a damp brush (*Fig. 4.10C*).

DRY BRUSH. Dip the sable brush in a rather thick color, then spread the hairs apart by pressing the brush down on the palette and rotating slightly (*Fig. 4.11A*). Lightly wipe off the excess color on a blotter or piece of paper, then drag the tips of the hairs across the drawing paper (*Fig. 4.11B*), with an upward motion at the end of the stroke. This is done in one direction. A light color can be drybrushed over a dark one and vice versa (*Figs. 4.12A* and *B*). Instead of two colors, three are used in *Fig. 4.12C*. Here the middle value is drybrushed into the dark, and

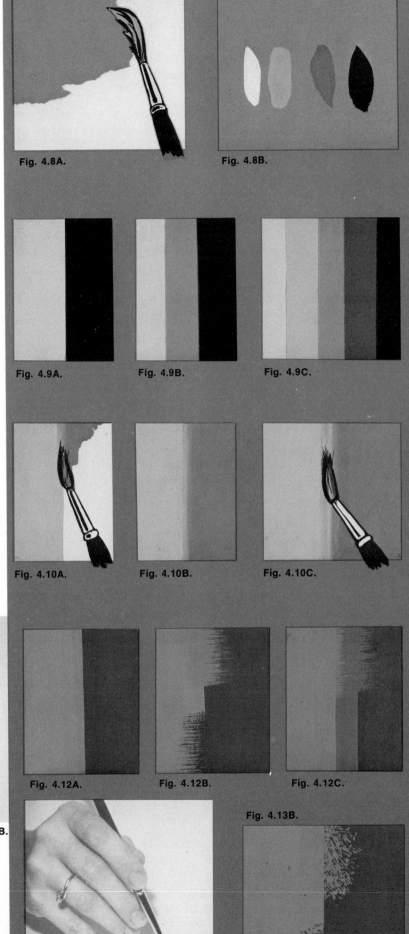

Fig. 4.8A. Fig. 4.8B.

Fig. 4.9A. Fig. 4.9B. Fig. 4.9C.

Fig. 4.10A. Fig. 4.10B. Fig. 4.10C.

Fig. 4.12A. Fig. 4.12B. Fig. 4.12C.

Fig. 4.13B.

Fig. 4.13A.

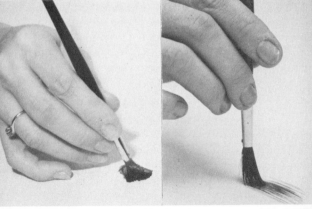

Fig. 4.11A. Fig. 4.11B.

then the light drybrushed into the middle value. A modified drybrush or semi-stipple is achieved by spreading the hairs apart, then tapping the paper gently with the brush held vertically (*Figs. 4.13A* and *B*), instead of rubbing it across the paper.

Fig. 4.14: Milton Herder.

Fig. 4.15: Hallmark Cards, Inc.

Fig. 4.16: Jeremiah Goodman, Lord & Taylor.

Examples of various artists' works are presented here to show the varied applications as well as the diversity of styles and techniques obtained with the same medium. Compare the finely textured effects in Howard Koslow's illustration with the loose, almost fluid quality of Geremiah's furniture illustration and the flat, simplified technique of the airline poster by McKnight Kauffer.

Howard Koslow is both a commercial illustrator and fine arts painter. His approach to both is the same insofar as the art is concerned, except that for the commercial assignments he has to consider the reproduction aspects as well as accuracy of subject portrayal and adherence to the objectives of the illustration. He works in acrylics, which provide excellent working control, laying a gesso ground with texture effects on illustration board or, for larger works, on masonite board. The basic abstract pattern characteristic of Koslow's work is first laid out broadly with a brush or painting knife, and then the structure is gradually refined and detail is added. Fast-drying acrylics, with their non-bleeding quality, are an asset in this respect. Drybrushing brings out the texture of the gesso ground and also allows the ground color to show through the overlying colors, creating a rich, vibrant painting quality. Koslow prefers to work with sable brushes, even though acrylics shorten their life considerably. Most commercial work is done about twice reproduction size; the paintings are done larger, about 2' x 3' in size.

Fig. 4.19: Howard Koslow

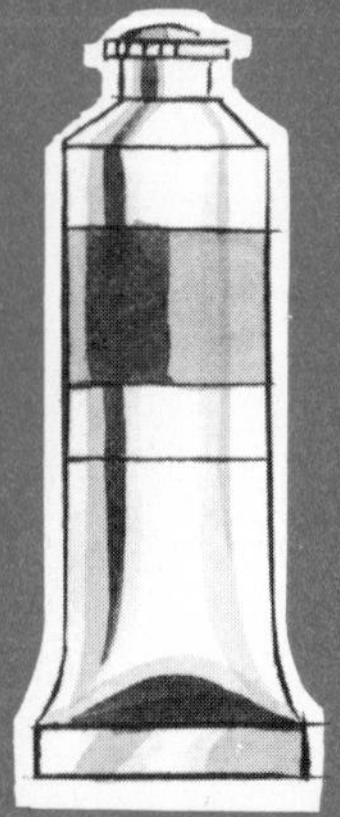

5. Transparent Watercolor and Wash

Fig. 5.1A:
Lampblack.

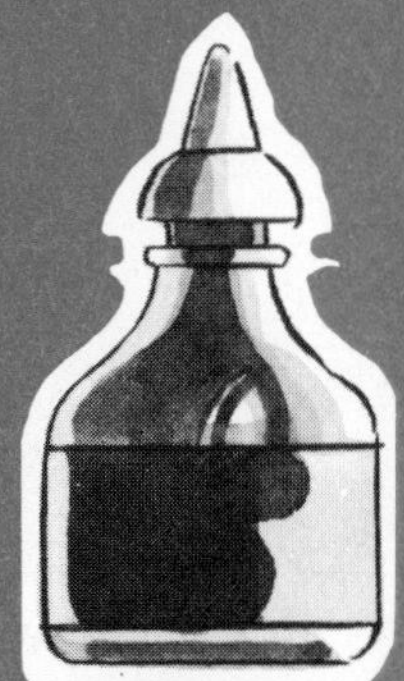

Fig. 5.1B:
India Ink.

Fig. 5.1C:
Chinese Stick Ink.

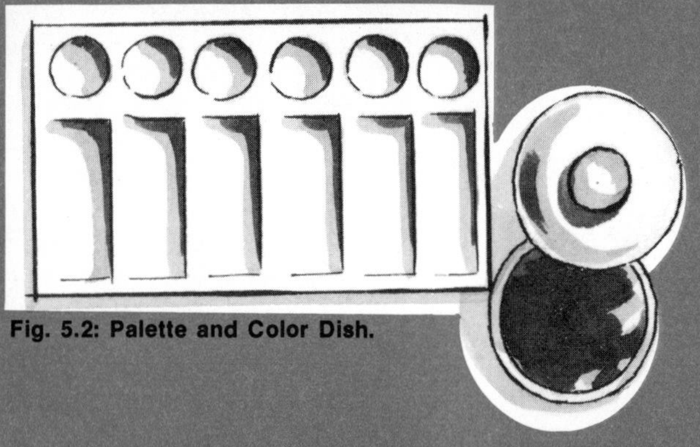

Fig. 5.2: Palette and Color Dish.

Fig. 5.3: Flat Sable Brush.

Fig. 5.4: Pointed Sable Brush.

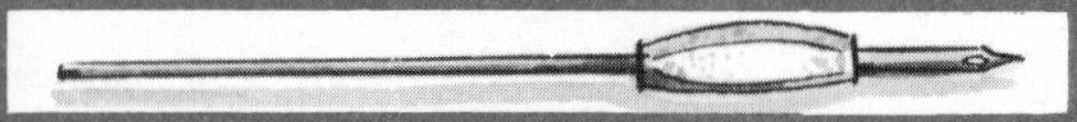

Fig. 5.5: Croquill Pen.

Fig. 5.6: Chinese Brush.

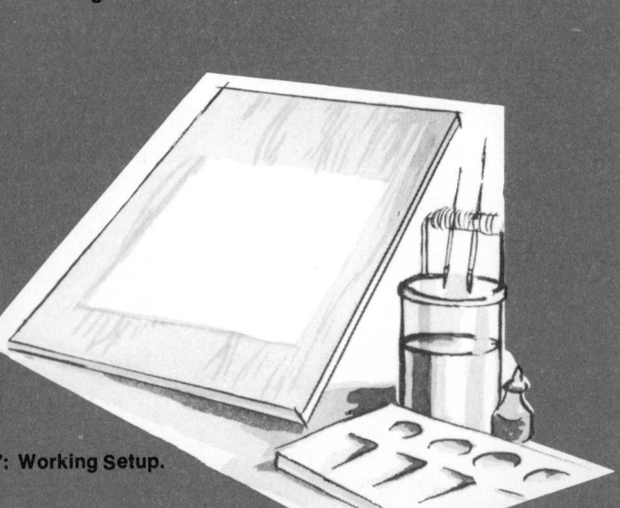

Fig. 5.7: Working Setup.

A WASH is an application of transparent watercolor. Gray tones can be made by diluting either lampblack, India ink, or Chinese stick ink. Lampblack is easiest to use, but India ink has the advantage of being waterproof, making it possible to lay one wash over another without picking up the one underneath. Chinese stick ink is prepared by rubbing the stick around in a porcelain dish with water until the desired amount is dissolved. This can be strained through a wet cloth to get rid of any solid particles that may be left. A concentrated solution of wash is made with any of the above materials and is best kept in a separate watercolor dish with a lid. This "mother wash" is diluted with water as required for lighter tones. The different strength washes may be kept in the same type of palette suggested for opaque watercolors, or in individual dishes.

The Application of Wash

Wash can be applied with round, pointed or flat, red sable brushes. Thin wash or ink lines can be drawn with a croquill pen or Chinese or Japanese brush. After use, brushes should always be rinsed out in clean water, pointed up carefully and laid flat where the hairs will not be disturbed. A combination brush holder and water jar like the one illustrated in *Fig. 5.7* is very handy. Any size brush fits into the spring holder, and the brush is left point downward. Brushes should be washed occasionally in warm water and mild soap, rubbing the brush gently in the palm of the hand, then rinsing it thoroughly in lukewarm water.

Only good watercolor paper or board, available in smooth or rough textured surfaces, should be used for wash drawings. Smooth paper is useful where detail is required; the rough paper for broad, bold effects. Very smooth paper is called "hot pressed"; rougher papers are called "cold pressed." Paper can be purchased in single sheets, pads or block form. The latter consists of a block of many sheets glued together around the edges. The sheet is removed when the painting is completed. "Board" is watercolor paper mounted on cardboard to prevent buckling. Paper is made in different thicknesses, known as "plys," and can range from one to several plys thick. The heavier papers are more durable and better to work on, but cost more.

FLAT WASH. To apply a wash, tape the paper to a drawing board tilted at about a 30-degree angle (*Fig. 5.7*). Load the brush with watercolor diluted to the desired value. Start at the top of the area to be covered, making an even, moderately fast stroke across the paper with the brush held quite flat so that most of the hairs touch the paper (*Fig. 5.8-1*). A pool of color will be carried along at the heel of the brush. A wash is floated on, not rubbed in. Upon reaching the end of the stroke (*Fig. 5.8-2*) bring the wash down without lifting the brush, and start back across the paper in the opposite direction, allowing a slight overlap with the previous stroke (*Fig. 5.8-3*). This is continued over the area to be covered. Before the brush loses its pool of color, quickly dip it into the palette and continue the next stroke. If you have too much wash left over at the end, pick it up with the tip of the brush after squeezing the brush dry.

GRADED WASH. To lay down a wash graded from dark to light value (*Fig. 5.9*), start out with the brush loaded with the dark tone, and dip it into clean water after every stroke or two, diluting it as you proceed downward.

SUPERIMPOSED WASHES. If a flat wash is applied and allowed to dry, as in *Fig. 5.10A*, and the same color lightly painted over part of it, as in *Fig. 5.10B*, the re-covered area will be darker. Another crossover with the same wash, *Fig. 5.10C*, will give a third value. Thus tones can be built up as desired by superimposed washes. If a stronger difference on the crossover is desired, a darker color is mixed for the overlap.

SOFTENING EDGES. When it is necessary to soften the edge of a wash which is being applied over a previous wash (*Fig. 5.11B*), rinse the brush out quickly in clean water and then (*Fig. 5.11C*) drag the tip slowly across the edge of the still wet wash. The brush should be held flat so that the water wets the paper a short distance below the wash, allowing the color to run down into it.

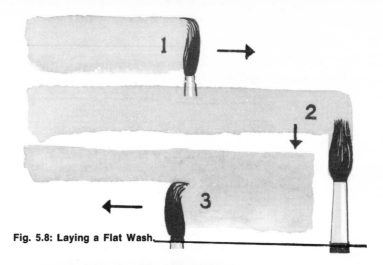

Fig. 5.8: Laying a Flat Wash.

Fig. 5.9: A Graded Wash.

Fig. 5.10: Superimposed Washes.

Fig. 5.11A.   Fig. 5.11B.   Fig. 5.11C:
Fig. 5.11: Softening an Edge.

Fig. 5.12.

COMBINATIONS. While not strictly a wash technique, it is possible and often advantageous to combine wash with pastel, charcoal or carbon pencil. The wash may be done first, then the other medium worked over it where small, controlled gradations are required. White pastel can be used for highlights. These overtones can be softened by smudging with the finger or a paper stump. Conversely, wash may be applied over a pencil or carbon drawing.

SOFT TONES. Very soft, fluid effects, characteristic of watercolor, can be obtained by working into a wet area. In the example in *Fig. 5.13*, the paper was first moistened with clear water, then a light wash was applied while the area was still wet. When the wash was nearly dry, the spots were dabbed in with a loaded brush. Working over wet paper increases the softness of the edges, but also decreases the control. When the wash is dry, sharp crisp accents can be added, as in the lower left. In a related method, the entire paper is soaked in water or wet with a sponge, then placed over wet newspaper to remain damp while being worked on.

Fig. 5.13.

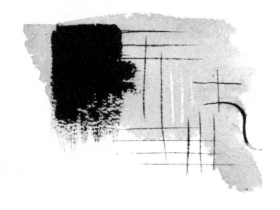

Fig. 5.14.

INK AND WASH. Combination ink and wash drawings (see pages 29 and 30) are quite effective. If waterproof India ink is used, the solid areas and linework can be done first with brush and pen, then either a flat or a graded wash worked over this. Further drawing in ink can be done after, if desired. White accents can be made with white poster paint or scraped out with a razor blade. Thin, lighter gray lines or dots can be secured by the use of retouch grays or black and white mixed to any value.

MASKING. Where the wash must terminate in a very sharp straight edge, masking tape can be used and the wash brushed right up to it. Don't allow the wash to collect along the tape and don't remove until both are dry. When they are dry pull the tape off slowly. A liquid masking medium called "Art Maskoid" can be brushed on the area to be protected from the wash. When it is dry, a wash can be brushed over it (*Fig. 5.15A*). After the wash is dry, the Maskoid is picked up by placing a piece of Scotch tape on the sticky surface and carefully lifting, leaving only the wash (*Fig. 5.15B*).

Fig. 5.15A.

Fig. 5.15B.

S. Ohrvel Carlson.

Fig. 5.18: Combination Ink and Watercolor Drawing.

The combination of pen line and wash drawing is a convenient and popular technique. When using waterproof ink, the ink drawing may be done first *Fig. 5.16*; then, after this has dried, the wash of diluted lampblack or diluted india ink may be applied with a watercolor brush of sable or related type, *Fig. 5.17*. Lighter tones are brushed on first, either following the ink drawing carefully, or merely using the ink drawing as a rough guide and brushing the wash on loosely. Successive washes may be built up to darken areas further, until the illustration is completed. Additional pen or brush and ink lines may be drawn in at this stage to emphasize or to complete it. This is a very convenient technique for sketching.

Fig. 5.16: The Pen and Ink Drawing.

Fig. 5.17: Applying Watercolor to an Ink Drawing.

Fig. 5.19: W. David Shaw, *Holiday Magazine.*

An effective combination of loose pen line and fluid wash technique is achieved in W. David Shaw's illustration reproduced above. After the line drawing was made with waterproof India ink, the lighter washes were applied with diluted ink. While these were still wet, or after having been dampened with water, the darker tones were brushed in and blended softly at the edges, as in the sky and water. Sharp-edged tones can be added when the surface is dry. This is an application of the wash techniques portrayed on pages 27 and 28. Shaw often uses a ruling pen and even a pipe cleaner dipped in ink as accessories to the croquill pen in drawing. The ruling pen is used in a freehand manner with the flat side, however, and twisted to create irregular lines and even broad strokes. This is difficult to control, though, and sometimes unhappy accidents occur.

Fig. 5.20: Greenhill, Lord & Taylor.

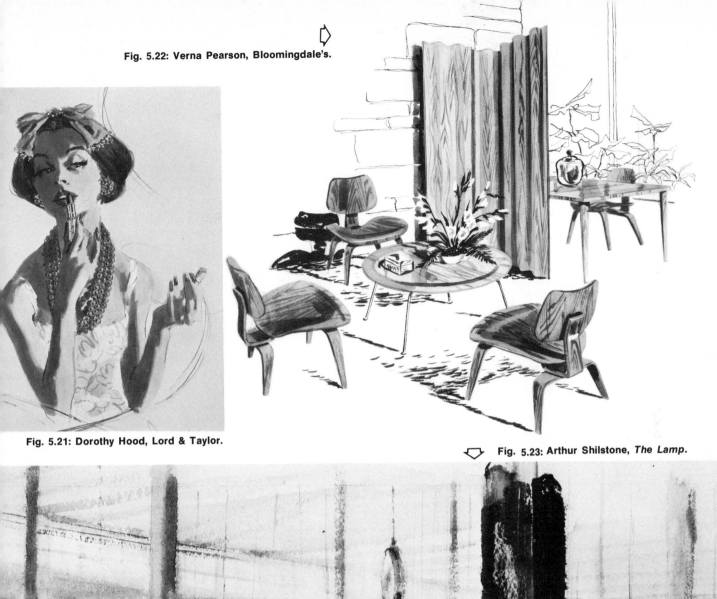

Fig. 5.22: Verna Pearson, Bloomingdale's.

Fig. 5.21: Dorothy Hood, Lord & Taylor.

Fig. 5.23: Arthur Shilstone, *The Lamp*.

6. Airbrush

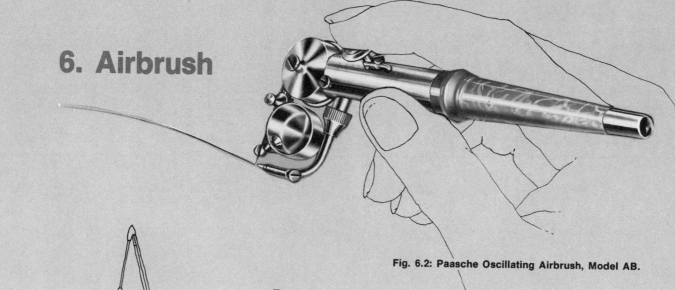

Fig. 6.2: Paasche Oscillating Airbrush, Model AB.

Fig. 6.1: Working Setup for Airbrush Painting.

THE AIRBRUSH is an instrument which enables the artist to spray paint over a surface with delicate and precise control. With the airbrush the artist can secure any variation from a pencil-thin line to a broad spray. Smooth, subtle gradations of tone are characteristic of airbrush art. Colors can be blended over each other without disturbing the ones underneath. Even controlled splatter or stipple effects are possible. The airbrush is excellent for rendering mechanical objects as well as pictorial effects. It is also used for architectural and product renderings, for schematic effects, technical illustration, photo retouching and coloring.

A practical working setup for airpainting is much the same as that used by any commercial artist, except that an air supply source is required (*Fig. 6.1*). This is obtained either by using a carbon dioxide tank, as illustrated, or by means of an air compressor. It is necessary to have adequate lighting, as shadows from the hand and airbrush on the artwork are very disturbing. A fluorescent "floating arm" lamp is ideal.

Fig. 6.4: Portable Air Compressor.

Fig. 6.3: Standard Double Action Airbrush.

The airbrush, when not in use, is suspended on a holder. This should be on the right side of the user to prevent dragging the hose across the lap while the airbrush is in use. If you are lefthanded, put the holder on your left. Airbrushes with the color cup on the left can be obtained for the convenience of left-handed artists. The tabouret and other utensils should also be to the right of the artist. A single pedestal, adjustable drawing table is easy and comfortable to work on. Most illustrative airbrush work is done at a board tilted at a 30- to 45-degree angle. It may be necessary, however, to have certain types of large work, such as displays, in a vertical position, in which case it is practical to work standing up. Do not keep your chair so close to the board that the action of your arms will be cramped, for it is necessary to be relaxed and unhampered.

Equipment and Materials

AIR SUPPLY. As the term "airbrush" implies, a source of air pressure is required to operate the brush. This is provided by means of either an air compressor or a carbon dioxide tank such as is used in soda fountains and is therefore easily obtainable. The air supply is connected to the airbrush by means of a rubber hose, and a regulator on the carbonic tank or compressor enables the artist to adjust the pressure to the proper working strength, which is about 25 pounds. The regulator and compressor must be purchased by the artist, but the carbonic gas tank can be rented. The 20-pound tank is the most practical size. When empty it can be replaced with another tank.

AIRBRUSHES. The "double-action" and oscillating types of airbrushes are used for artwork and photo retouching (*Fig. 6.2*). The double action brush is applicable for general studio work, including fine work (*Fig. 6.3*). The oscillating type is excellent for fine work only; it is slower acting and allows for easier control in delicate airbrushing. The three major models of airbrushes for general studio work are the Thayer Chandler Model A, the Paasche VI, and the Wold A. The most popular oscillating type is the Paasche AB model. Properly cared for, an airbrush will last a lifetime, with only occasional replacement parts necessary.

PIGMENTS. Any finely ground water soluble pigment, alcohol color or aniline dye can be used in the airbrush. These can be either transparent or opaque color. Opaque grays, of the type discussed on page 21, are used for both photo retouching and rendering. These may be obtained in tubes or jars, in sets of approximately six scaled values of neutral grays, from very light to dark. Other retouch grays are made in warm (brownish) tones and cool (bluish) tones for retouching photos.

PAPER. Any good watercolor board or heavy paper can be used for airbrush art. Do not use too rough a paper if fine detail is required. Hot pressed paper is a beautiful surface for mechanical subjects done in transparent watercolor but must be handled gingerly, as abrasions or grease will affect airbrushing.

OTHER MATERIALS. Areas not to be sprayed are covered with masks made of drawing paper, stencil paper or acetate. Intricate areas are managed by adhering frisket paper (see page 36) to the drawing with rubber cement and cutting out the areas to be airbrushed. A frisket knife is used for the cutting.

A rubber cement dispenser, a palette, red sable brushes and the usual drawing or drafting instruments complete the list of supplies.

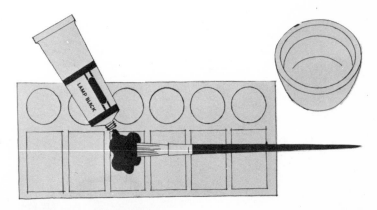

Fig. 6.5: Airbrush Pigments, Dyes and Palette for Color Mixing.

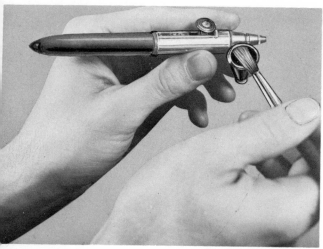

Fig. 6.6: Fill Color Cup.

Operating the Airbrush

We shall start with lampblack used transparently, as our pigment (*Fig. 6.5*). (The information on the characteristics of opaque and transparent color given at the beginning of the chapter on Opaque Watercolor is applicable to the airbrush.)

Dilute the lampblack with water to approximate the consistency used to secure a medium value wash, and fill the color cup with it (*Fig. 6.6*). A long haired bristle brush or eyedropper is useful for this purpose. Do not use a brush that will shed hairs, as they will get into the airbrush and clog it.

With the hand held about eight inches away from the paper, start moving it across the paper from right to left in a slow but deliberate movement, keeping it at the same level (*Fig. 6.7*). The brush should be pointed almost at right angles to the paper, remaining so throughout the length of the stroke. Move the hand and forearm across the page without bending the wrist. The movement should be from the shoulder. After the hand has traveled two or three inches, press down the trigger, all the way (*Fig. 6.8*). This action releases only the air, not the paint. Do this without stopping or slowing down the movement of the hand across the page. All actions must be smooth and coordinated.

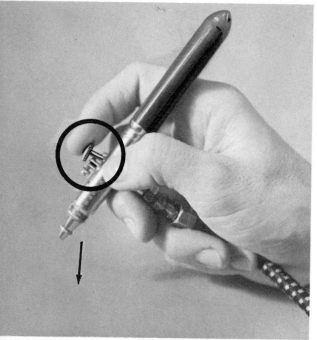

Fig. 6.7: Start Hand Movement.

Fig. 6.8: Press Trigger Down.

Now, with the trigger still held down, pull back on the trigger, slowly and evenly, releasing the paint (*Fig. 6.9*). The paint should not start out in an abrupt spurt, but should come out gradually. (Remember, your hand is still moving slowly across the page.)

The amount of paint issuing from the brush is governed by the extent to which the trigger is pulled back. The paint should dry almost upon touching the paper; if it puddles or fans out in streamlets you are pulling back too far on the trigger or are working too close to the paper.

Approaching the end of the stroke, allow the trigger to move forward to its starting position (*Fig. 6.10*), so that the paint flow is gradually cut off. Then stop the motion of the hand.

Now start the next stroke back in the opposite direction (*Fig. 6.11*), following exactly the same procedure as before. Allow the spray to overlap the previous one along the edge.

Continue these alternate strokes down the page until the area is covered with a flat, even tone of color. Then stop airflow from brush by releasing pressure on the trigger (*Fig. 6.11*).

Airbrushed tones are built up gradually. To obtain a dark, flat wash airpaint over the area, starting at the top and repeating until the desired tone is obtained.

A graded wash is best secured if you start at the bottom of the area and allow it to fade out near the top on the first passage; then start at the bottom again, but do not take the spray up quite as far as on the previous passage. Repeat this until the required gradation is built up. See the illustrations of this as applied to the rendering of a cube (page 37).

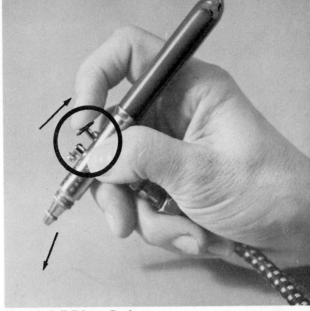

Fig. 6.9: Pull Trigger Back.

Fig. 6.10: Push Trigger Forward.

Fig. 6.11: Release Trigger Up.

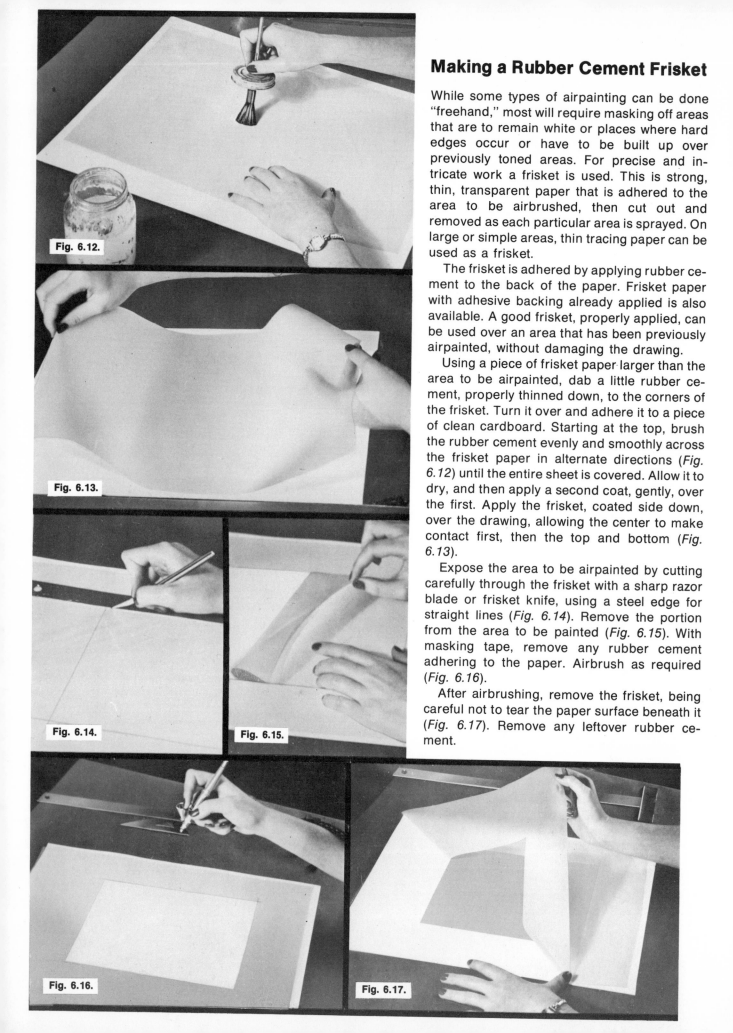

Making a Rubber Cement Frisket

While some types of airpainting can be done "freehand," most will require masking off areas that are to remain white or places where hard edges occur or have to be built up over previously toned areas. For precise and intricate work a frisket is used. This is strong, thin, transparent paper that is adhered to the area to be airbrushed, then cut out and removed as each particular area is sprayed. On large or simple areas, thin tracing paper can be used as a frisket.

The frisket is adhered by applying rubber cement to the back of the paper. Frisket paper with adhesive backing already applied is also available. A good frisket, properly applied, can be used over an area that has been previously airpainted, without damaging the drawing.

Using a piece of frisket paper larger than the area to be airpainted, dab a little rubber cement, properly thinned down, to the corners of the frisket. Turn it over and adhere it to a piece of clean cardboard. Starting at the top, brush the rubber cement evenly and smoothly across the frisket paper in alternate directions (*Fig. 6.12*) until the entire sheet is covered. Allow it to dry, and then apply a second coat, gently, over the first. Apply the frisket, coated side down, over the drawing, allowing the center to make contact first, then the top and bottom (*Fig. 6.13*).

Expose the area to be airpainted by cutting carefully through the frisket with a sharp razor blade or frisket knife, using a steel edge for straight lines (*Fig. 6.14*). Remove the portion from the area to be painted (*Fig. 6.15*). With masking tape, remove any rubber cement adhering to the paper. Airbrush as required (*Fig. 6.16*).

After airbrushing, remove the frisket, being careful not to tear the paper surface beneath it (*Fig. 6.17*). Remove any leftover rubber cement.

Fig. 6.12.

Fig. 6.13.

Fig. 6.14.

Fig. 6.15.

Fig. 6.16.

Fig. 6.17.

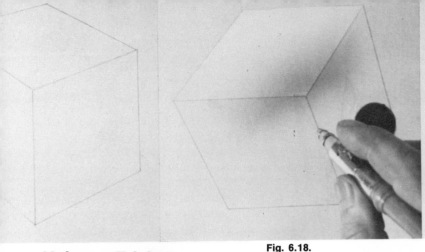

Fig. 6.18.

Fig. 6.18A.

Using a Frisket

In this exercise, an accurate pencil outline drawing of a cube is entirely covered with a frisket, and the frisket removed from the plane that is to be darkest. The drawing is turned so that the corner to be darkest is nearest to you.

Starting at this corner airbrush a tone across the plane, allowing it to fade out at the opposite corner (*Fig. 6.18*). Return to the near corner and repeat the procedure. Continue this until a solid black has been built up in this corner fading out to the opposite corner, as shown in *Fig. 6.18A*. In *Fig. 6.19* the frisket has been removed from the second plane to be rendered, the beginning of which is shown. Do not worry about any slight spillover of paint on

Fig. 6.19A.

g. 6.19. the plane already shaded, as it is so dark that the slight spillover will not show. This is the reason for starting with the darkest plane in this case, as well as because subsequent values can be "keyed" to this darkest area. This second plane is covered like the first, except that it is left lighter overall (*Fig. 6.18A*).

Now the frisket is removed from the last plane (*Fig. 6.20*), and again a graded wash applied, still lighter than on the second plane.

No pigment is applied to the far corner, so that it will remain white. The frisket is now removed from the area surrounding the drawing, and any rubber cement left on the paper removed with a rubber cement pickup.

The completed cube is shown right side up in *Fig. 6.20A*. In all other illustrations on this page it was shown from the angle at which you would view it while doing the work.

Fig. 6.20A.

g. 6.20.

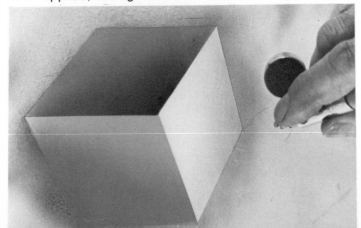

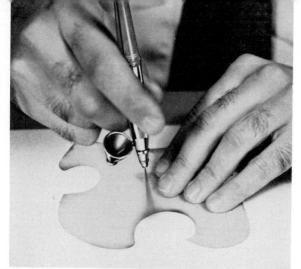

Fig. 6.21.

Fig. 6.22.

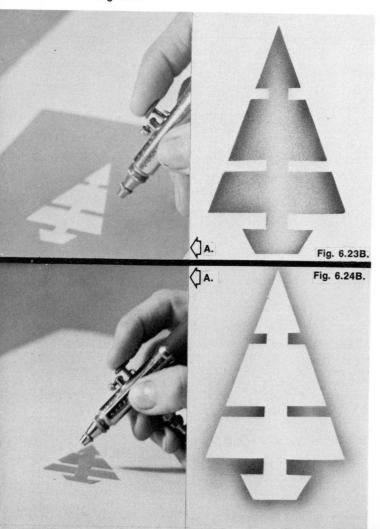

A.

Fig. 6.23B.

A.

Fig. 6.24B.

Masks

Various shaped masks made of acetate or drawing paper can be used to advantage in air-brush work. A mask serves the same purpose as a frisket except that it is not rubber-cemented to the drawing, but is used as a loose, movable shield which can be adjusted to the shape of the area to be protected. It is advisable to keep on hand a number of masks with different curves and angles. These can be made by scoring the acetate lightly with a razor blade and then carefully bending the acetate along the cut. The edge of the cut can be smoothed with sandpaper so that a free-flowing curve and clean-cut edge will result.

If the mask is held in contact with the paper, as in *Fig. 6.21*, and a tone airbrushed over its edge, the airbrushing will conform to the shape of the mask. This can be seen in *Fig. 6.22*, where the mask has been pulled back from its position at A, where it had been held during air-brushing. Note that the edge of the airbrushed area is sharp where it was in contact with the mask and then fades out softly.

When a soft rather than a sharp edge is required, the mask can be lifted from the paper and allowed to rest on a thick, flat ruler during airpainting. The more vertically the brush is held while doing this, the sharper will be the tone nearest the edge of the mask.

Stencils

When it is necessary to duplicate a design or when it is inconvenient to make a frisket, a stencil can be cut from stencil or drawing paper and used as a shield for airbrushing. In *Fig. 6.23A* a Christmas tree shape has been cut out and removed from the stencil. Airbrushing along the edge of this cutout will give the result shown in *Fig. 6.23B*. When using a mask or stencil in airbrushing, it is advisable to airbrush *over* the edge of the stencil rather than *into* the edge. Otherwise the paint will creep beneath the edge of the stencil and not give a clean-cut result.

For a reverse effect the portion cut out from the stencil in the previous illustration can be used as a mask to achieve the result shown in *Fig. 6.24B*. Again care must be taken to air-brush off the edge of the mask (*Fig. 6.24A*) rather than into the edge. It is possible to combine several stencils to build up a completely shaded illustration where it is necessary to repeat the motif, as on textiles, greeting cards and airbrush paintings.

Airbrush Line Work

The following exercises are designed to teach three skills: how to direct the pattern where desired; how to judge the proper distance between hand and paper; how to determine how far to pull back on the finger lever. The distance between hand and paper and the amount the finger lever is pulled back govern the size of the spray pattern.

BROAD LINE. With a pencil, rule off on drawing paper a series of horizontal lines about one inch apart. Starting with the top line and holding the airbrush about *five inches* from the paper in a vertical position, aim the airbrush at the line so that the spray pattern will be centered over it. Pull back on the finger lever far enough to give a very broad pattern about two inches in width (*Fig. 6.25*). Proceed evenly across the page, following the line. Release the paint and air at the end of the stroke. Repeat this in the opposite direction on the second pencil line. Continue until the page is covered.

MEDIUM LINE. Using a clean sheet of paper ruled off in the same manner, hold the brush about *two inches* from the paper and, again directing the pattern at the center of the line, airbrush a pattern about a quarter of an inch wide across the paper (*Fig. 6.26*). The finger lever will not be pulled back as far as in the previous one. It is necessary to acquire proper coordination between the pull on the finger lever and the distance from the paper and consistently to pull back the same distance on the lever.

FINE LINE. Holding the brush as close to the paper as possible and pulling back very, very slightly on the lever, try to follow the pencil line carefully with a pattern of about the same width (*Fig. 6.27*).

Fig. 6.25: Broad Line.

Fig. 6.26: Medium Line.

Fig. 6.27: Fine Line.

Airbrushed Illustration

A step-by-step sequence in executing a relatively simple airbrush illustration is shown on these two pages. Airbrush art often requires supplementary techniques such as ruling pen and brush linework and lettering. The way in which these can be incorporated in airbrush procedures is shown here. Though a preliminary sketch was made before starting this visual, it is not shown; however, examination of the finished illustration (*Fig. 6.39*) will be helpful in understanding the sequence. This visual was prepared as a title card for black-and-white TV, provision having to be made to "super" various credits on the background (see page 121 for TV procedures). Since the airbrushing in this illustration was done with transparent black watercolor, the linework was done first. Gray TV illustration board was used. The 6" x 9" usable TV area of the drawing was done on an 11" x 14" board. The TV mask shown in the finished illustration was used only as a guide for size.

An accurate pencil outline is made on tracing paper, then transferred to gray TV board using white chalk on the back of the tracing (*Fig. 6.28*).

Linework is executed with a ruling pen and number three retouch gray opaque watercolor. The T-square is used with the pen (*Fig. 6.29* and *6.30*).

The letter "R" is brushed in with opaque gray (*Fig. 6.31*). The linework is completed (*Fig. 6.32*). The drawing is now ready for air-brushing.

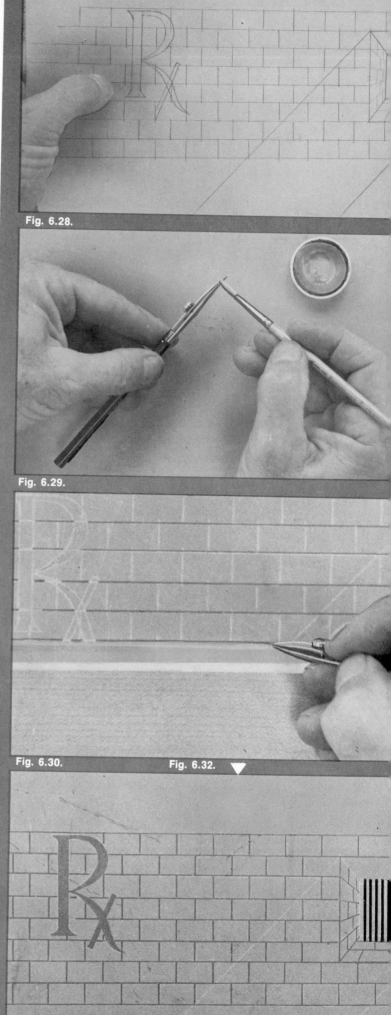

Fig. 6.28.

Fig. 6.29.

Fig. 6.30.

Fig. 6.32. ▼

▼ Fig. 6.31.

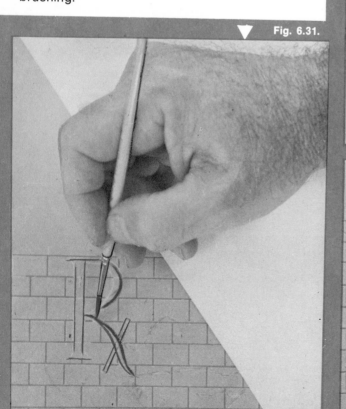

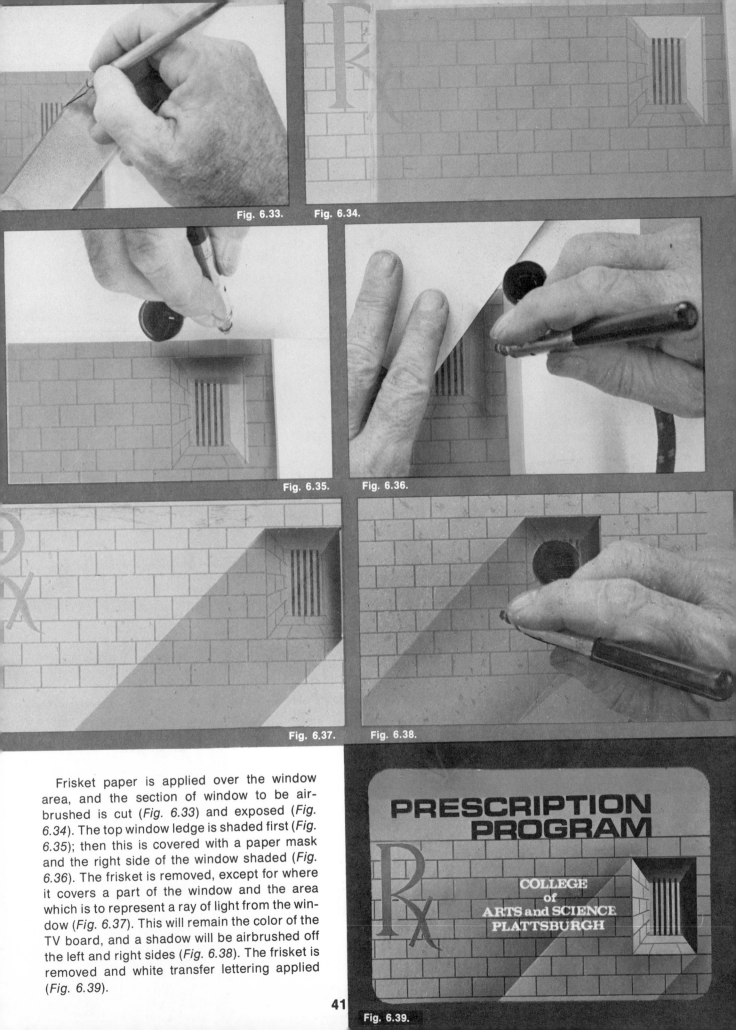

Fig. 6.33. Fig. 6.34.

Fig. 6.35. Fig. 6.36.

Fig. 6.37. Fig. 6.38.

Frisket paper is applied over the window area, and the section of window to be airbrushed is cut (*Fig. 6.33*) and exposed (*Fig. 6.34*). The top window ledge is shaded first (*Fig. 6.35*); then this is covered with a paper mask and the right side of the window shaded (*Fig. 6.36*). The frisket is removed, except for where it covers a part of the window and the area which is to represent a ray of light from the window (*Fig. 6.37*). This will remain the color of the TV board, and a shadow will be airbrushed off the left and right sides (*Fig. 6.38*). The frisket is removed and white transfer lettering applied (*Fig. 6.39*).

41

PRESCRIPTION PROGRAM

℞

COLLEGE
of
ARTS and SCIENCE
PLATTSBURGH

Fig. 6.39.

Fig. 6.40: H. K. Wimmer, Young & Rubican Advertising Agency.

Subtle tonal gradations and the rendering of three-dimensional form are characteristic of airbrush-work. Its versatility is also shown in such diverse applications as the stylized ski poster *(Fig. 6.42)* and the realistic, mechanical rendering of the motor *(Fig. 6.44)*.

The effect in *Fig. 6.41C* was cleverly achieved by crumpling a sheet of paper, then partly smoothing it out and airbrushing over it at a low angle so that one side of the wrinkles caught the paint and the opposite side did not. When flattened out completely and pasted down, the sheet still gives the appearance of being crumpled *(Fig. 6.41A)*. The remainder of the artwork was pasted on an overlay *(Fig. 6.41B)* to provide the combined finish and color separation drawings.

Fig. 6.41: Milton Herder, Doubleday & Co.

manning coles

not negotiable

not negotiable

doubleday   **manning coles**

Fig. 6.42.

Fig. 6.43: Bart Forbes, Kimberly-Clark Corp.

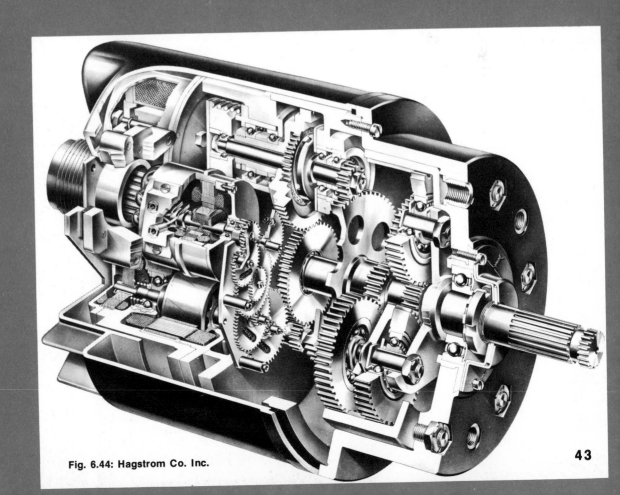

Fig. 6.44: Hagstrom Co. Inc.

43

7. Pastel

Fig. 7.1: Milton Herder.

PASTEL IS DRY PIGMENT mixed with a binder and compressed into stick or pencil form. It is an excellent medium for illustrative sketches (*Fig. 7.1*), renderings (*Fig. 7.3*) and layouts (*Fig. 7.4*).

Materials

PASTELS. Pastel is made in soft, medium and hard grades; the latter in square stick form (*Fig. 7.5*), the others in cylindrical stick and pencil form (*Fig. 7.6*). Since pastel is almost pure pigment, it can be obtained in extremely brilliant colors as well as subdued hues. It can be purchased in various size sets or individual sticks. The hard pastels are also made in sets of grays of different values, including black and white. Known as "layout chalks," these are useful where specific tones of gray are desirable.

PAPER. Pastel paper is usually gray or colored, as both the light and dark colors contrast well against such a background. The paper should have a slight "tooth." Certain papers or brands are made specifically for the use of pastel, some with a velour surface or fine sandpaper surface, to which pastel adheres very well. Pastel also adheres well to charcoal and tracing papers.

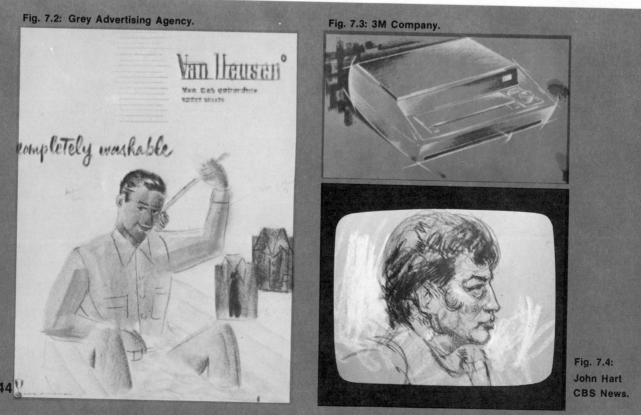

Fig. 7.2: Grey Advertising Agency.

Fig. 7.3: 3M Company.

Fig. 7.4: John Hart CBS News.

Characteristics and Techniques

Pastel is applied directly to the paper, using the end of the stick for line effects and the side of the stick for broad strokes or flat overall tones.

HARD PASTEL. Hard pastel can be sharpened to a rather fine point for detail drawings (*Fig. 7.7*) or the end can be left square or sharpened to a wedge shape for strokes up to a quarter of an inch wide. Pastel drawings are often built up with short strokes (*Fig. 7.2*), with one or more overlapping colors which blend together visually. Hard pastels have a glossy coating which should be sandpapered or shaved off when using the side of the stick.

SOFT PASTEL. *Fig. 7.8A* shows soft pastel being used on its side for a broad stroke. Large areas of color can be applied in this manner. Colors can be applied so that they leave sharp edges, as at 1, or a soft edge, 2, by keeping one end of the pastel raised slightly during the stroke. A darker color can be applied over a lighter one in this manner, 3.

Blending and softening of edges can also be done with the finger or a paper stump. Details can be drawn on the large masses with pointed hard pastels. Black chalk and charcoal pencils can also be used for details as they blend easily with the pastel.

SPECIAL TECHNIQUES. When crisp, irregular shapes are required, for example when making layouts or dummies, a stencil can be cut from tracing paper with a sharp razor blade (*Fig. 7.9A*) and used as a mask. The direction of the pastel stroke should be away from or along the edge of the mask rather than toward it; otherwise the mask will be ineffective. It is necessary sometimes to hold down an edge of the mask with drafting tape, as indicated in the lower lefthand corner. The effect obtained with this particular mask is shown in *Fig. 7.9B*. Two straight pieces of paper, held at right angles, were used as masks to work the pastel into a sharp corner.

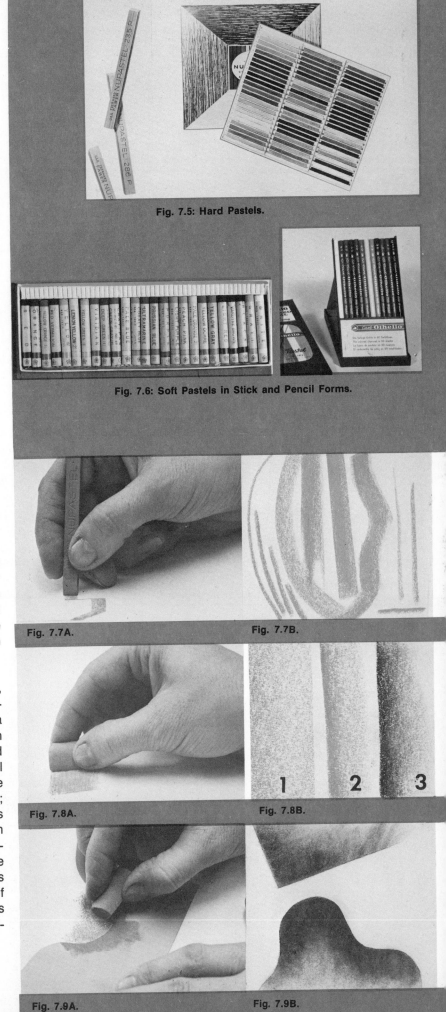

Fig. 7.5: Hard Pastels.

Fig. 7.6: Soft Pastels in Stick and Pencil Forms.

Fig. 7.7A.

Fig. 7.7B.

Fig. 7.8A.

Fig. 7.8B.

Fig. 7.9A.

Fig. 7.9B.

8. Pen and Ink

THE "LINE" MEDIA presented in this part of the book provide a different execution problem from the "continuous tone" media, previously considered. When working with line media the range of tones from black to the very lightest gray has to be obtained through the use of pure black only, that is, no *actual* gray tones are used. This is achieved by the use of lines or dots or configurations which, while solid black in themselves, give the appearance of gray tones through their variation in size and arrangement. However, there are many different ways of handling pen or brush and ink; furthermore, many different techniques are possible, through the choice of drawing instruments and the manner in which they are used by the artist.

Equipment and Materials

Some of the many tools for ink drawing are illustrated on the next page. Each is particularly suited to specific uses or effects. Even such objects as a pipe stem cleaner or a wooden splinter can be put to good use for loose, irregular effects, as are ballpoint writing pens.

PAPER. Almost any paper will accept ink; even blotting paper provides an interesting spread-line effect, if that is desired. However, the tool must suit the surface; a steel pen point would have to be handled very carefully on a rough watercolor paper, whereas a bamboo pen would be ideal for the purpose. For a clean, crisp pen line, a smooth, hard paper or board such as hot pressed bristol is excellent. Kid finish illustration or bristol board or heavy drawing papers are good for a softer line. Newsprint will give an irregular line that "blots" where the pen is stopped for a moment. Bond paper is good for quick sketches.

INK. Black India ink, both waterproof and nonwaterproof, colored inks and dyes, inks for use on acetate (generally used for overlays and color separations) and Chinese stick ink may be used with pens or brushes. Most felt and nylon tip pens utilize liquid dyes which can fade on prolonged exposure to sunlight and some of which spread rather rapidly on the paper, making a very fine line difficult to obtain, but such pens are very handy to use and are receptive to any paper surface.

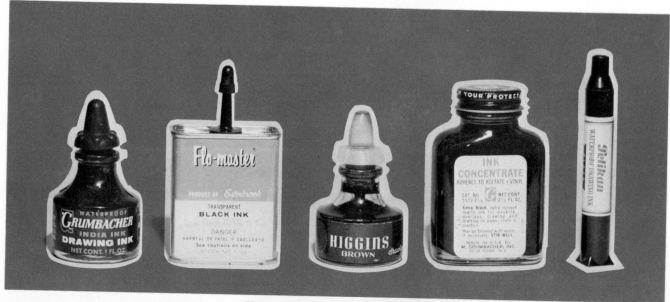

Fig. 8.1: Various Types of Inks and Dyes.

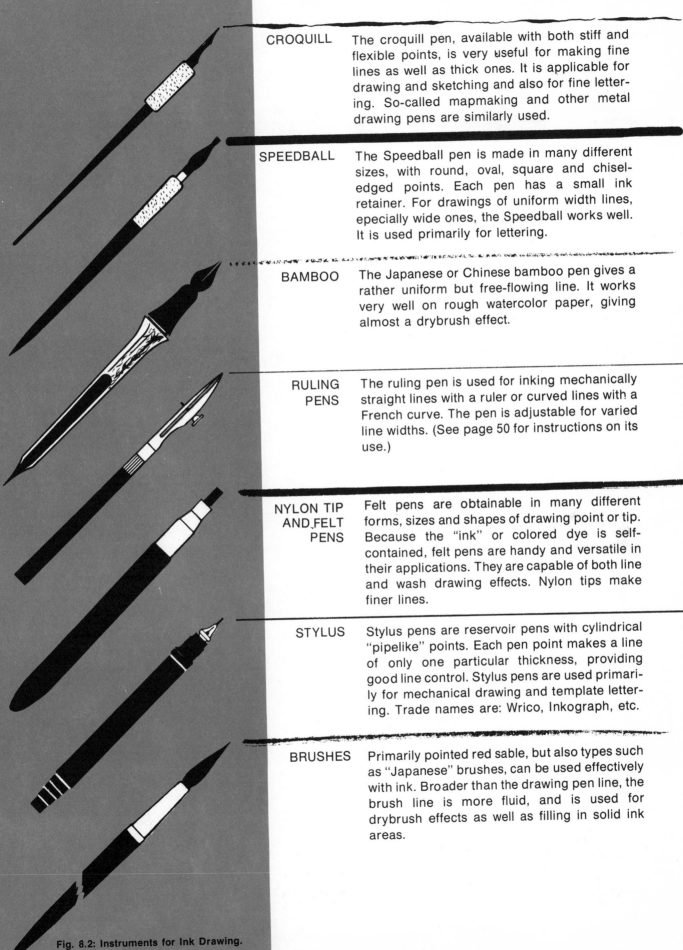

PENS

CROQUILL The croquill pen, available with both stiff and flexible points, is very useful for making fine lines as well as thick ones. It is applicable for drawing and sketching and also for fine lettering. So-called mapmaking and other metal drawing pens are similarly used.

SPEEDBALL The Speedball pen is made in many different sizes, with round, oval, square and chisel-edged points. Each pen has a small ink retainer. For drawings of uniform width lines, epecially wide ones, the Speedball works well. It is used primarily for lettering.

BAMBOO The Japanese or Chinese bamboo pen gives a rather uniform but free-flowing line. It works very well on rough watercolor paper, giving almost a drybrush effect.

RULING PENS The ruling pen is used for inking mechanically straight lines with a ruler or curved lines with a French curve. The pen is adjustable for varied line widths. (See page 50 for instructions on its use.)

NYLON TIP AND FELT PENS Felt pens are obtainable in many different forms, sizes and shapes of drawing point or tip. Because the "ink" or colored dye is self-contained, felt pens are handy and versatile in their applications. They are capable of both line and wash drawing effects. Nylon tips make finer lines.

STYLUS Stylus pens are reservoir pens with cylindrical "pipelike" points. Each pen point makes a line of only one particular thickness, providing good line control. Stylus pens are used primarily for mechanical drawing and template lettering. Trade names are: Wrico, Inkograph, etc.

BRUSHES Primarily pointed red sable, but also types such as "Japanese" brushes, can be used effectively with ink. Broader than the drawing pen line, the brush line is more fluid, and is used for drybrush effects as well as filling in solid ink areas.

Fig. 8.2: Instruments for Ink Drawing.

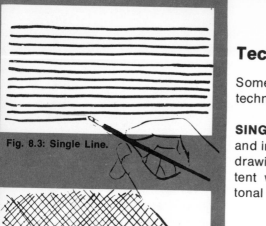

Fig. 8.3: Single Line.

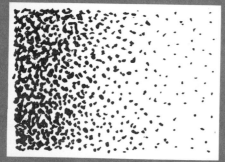

Fig. 8.4: Cross-Hatch.

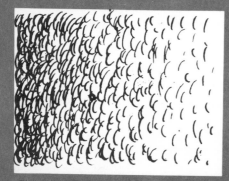

Fig. 8.5: Stipple.

Fig. 8.6: Free Technique.

Fig. 8.7: Graded Line.

Anna Marie Magagna.

Techniques

Some of the more common pen and ink techniques are identified here.

SINGLE LINE. The simplest type of pen and ink technique is the free-hand outline drawing done with a single line of consistent width. By drawing parallel lines, a tonal effect can be achieved (*Fig. 8.3*).

Sir Robert Burnett Co.

CROSS-HATCHING. By crossing lines at right angles, or some other angle, a crosshatch is obtained, which breaks up the parallel line effect of *Fig. 8.3* and provides more opportunity for tone and texture effects (*Fig. 8.4*).

John Arvan, *Ford Times*.

STIPPLING. A stipple consists of dots which give different values by their size and placement (*Fig. 8.5*). A variation of the stipple begins to approach the line effect in the free technique shown in *Fig. 8.7*.

Al Hirshfeld, *The New York Times*.

SHADING TECHNIQUES. The "shading" techniques—used when a variation in tone is desired in a given area—can be broken down into two types: those in which a line or dot of consistent width is used (*Figs. 8.8* and *8.11*), and those in which the size of the lines or dots are graded or varied in size within the same drawing (*Figs. 8.6* and *8.9*). Straight or curved lines of consistent width may be drawn parallel to each other over an area to give the effect of a flat tone. The tonal effects may be varied by changing the thickness of the lines and their spacing, as shown on the next page.

In all these techniques, care must be taken to keep any line or dot, no matter how fine, solid black; otherwise, it will not reproduce properly.

Rockwell Kent,

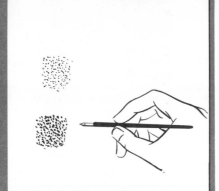

Fig. 8.8: Stipple—Flat Values.

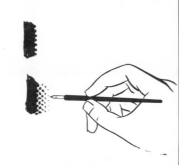

Fig. 8.9: Graded Stipple—Mechanical.

Fig. 8.10: Graded Stipple—Free.

Black dots drawn with a pen, freely or mechanically, can be controlled to indicate various degrees of value: heavy dots drawn close together for a dark value; light dots further apart for a light value. A transition from solid black to white can be made by stippling out from the black area with pen or brush. Note that the dots are drawn smaller and further apart as the value is lightened.

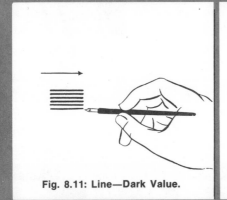

Fig. 8.11: Line—Dark Value.

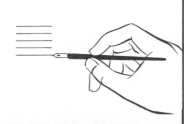

Fig. 8.12: Line—Light Value.

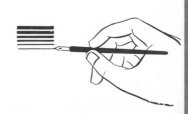

Fig. 8.13: Graded Tone.

Heavy lines close together give dark value (*Fig. 8.11*). Note that the pen is held parallel to the line being drawn. The line is a continuation of the axis of the pen. This, of course, cannot be maintained for curved lines of short radius, but is an advantage when drawing "graded" lines as shown below. Thin lines further apart give a light value (*Fig. 8.12*). As black lines are made thinner, the white spaces between are increased, giving a tone graded from dark to light (*Fig. 8.13*).

The lines themselves can be graded from thin to thick by increasing the pressure evenly on the pen while drawing the line (*Fig. 8.14*). To secure mechanically straight, graded lines, the drawing pen can be used against a metal-edged ruler, which is placed upside down so the metal edge is high enough to touch the pen point on the body of the nib (*Figs. 8.15-8.16*).

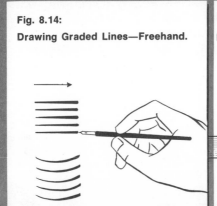

Fig. 8.14:
Drawing Graded Lines—Freehand.

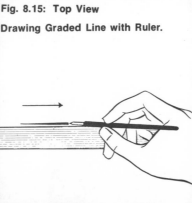

Fig. 8.15: Top View
Drawing Graded Line with Ruler.

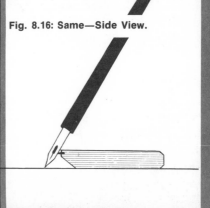

Fig. 8.16: Same—Side View.

Use of Drawing Instruments

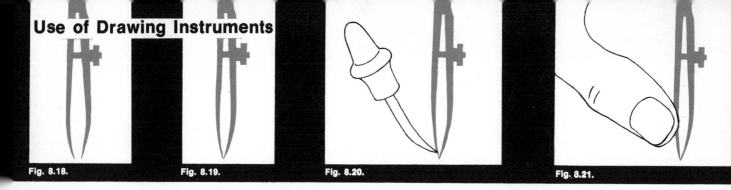

Fig. 8.18. Fig. 8.19. Fig. 8.20. Fig. 8.21.

USE OF RULING PEN. The ruling pen is used with ink or opaque watercolor to make mechanically straight or curved lines of uniform thickness. The thickness of the line can be varied by adjusting the position of the blade prongs of the pen with the nut. In the open posi- tion it will give a thick pen line (*Fig. 8.18*); in the closed position it will give a thin pen line (*Fig. 8.19*); variations between these extremes are possible. Fill the pen with India ink by means of the filler attached to the bottle stopper (*Fig. 8.20*). Wipe off the excess ink (*Fig. 8.21*).

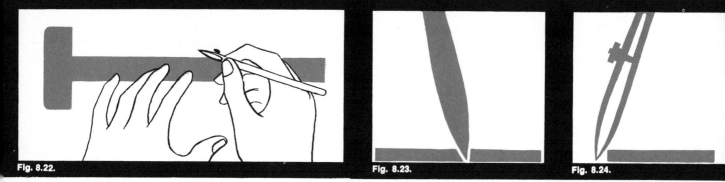

Fig. 8.22. Fig. 8.23. Fig. 8.24.

The pen is used against the side of a T-square for straight lines (*Fig. 8.22*). The front view (*Fig. 8.23*) taken from A, and the side view (*Fig. 8.24*), taken from B, will clarify the positions of the pen. The same pen angle should be maintained throughout the stroke.

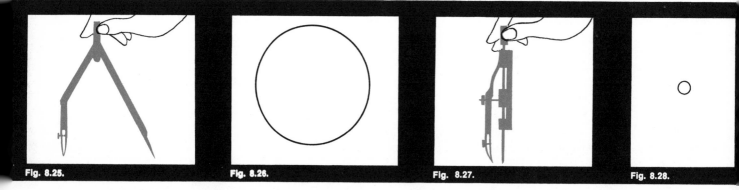

Fig. 8.25. Fig. 8.26. Fig. 8.27. Fig. 8.28.

USE OF PEN COMPASS. The pen compass (*Fig. 8.25*) is used to make circles (*Fig. 8.26*). The "drop compass" (*Fig. 8.27*) is used for very small circles (*Fig. 8.28*). The ruling pen is used with a "French curve" (*Fig. 8.29*) to make ac- curate curved lines. It can also be used with an "adjustable curve" (*Fig. 8.30*) which can be shaped as required.

Fig. 8.29. Fig. 8.30.

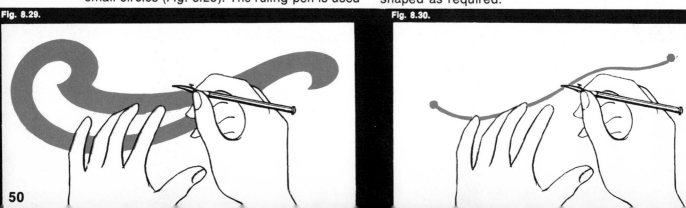

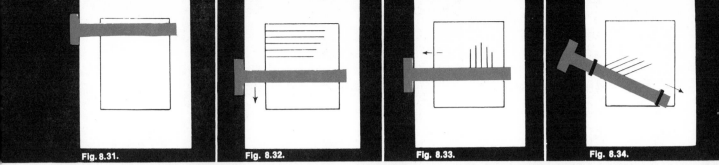

Fig. 8.31.   Fig. 8.32.   Fig. 8.33.   Fig. 8.34.

USE OF T-SQUARE AND TRIANGLE.

With the T-square held firmly against the left side of the drawing board, line up the top of the drawing paper with the top edge of the T-square (*Fig. 8.31*). The T-square can thus be lowered to any position for ruling horizontal parallel lines (*Fig. 8.32*). For ruling vertical lines, use the vertical side of the triangle as a guide (*Fig. 8.33*). For ruling parallel lines at other angles, adjust the triangle to the desired line, set the T-square against the base of the triangle, and then slide the triangle along the T-square in this position (*Fig. 8.34*).

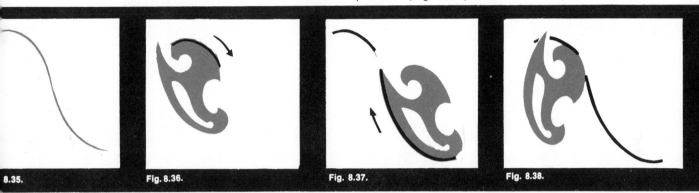

8.35.   Fig. 8.36.   Fig. 8.37.   Fig. 8.38.

USE OF FRENCH CURVE.

A curved line which is to be drawn accurately and smoothly with the French curve is first sketched lightly in pencil (*Fig. 8.35*). Fit a corresponding section of the French curve to the line at A and follow the curve with a pencil (*Fig. 8.36*). Move the French curve to B and draw this section of the line (*Fig. 8.37*). Now join A and B with section C, completing the drawing of the curved line (*Fig. 8.38*). Pen and ink can be used.

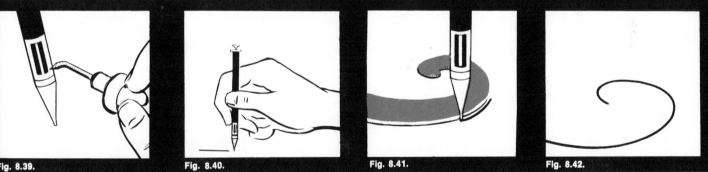

Fig. 8.39.   Fig. 8.40.   Fig. 8.41.   Fig. 8.42.

DRAWING ELLIPSES.

The stylus pen makes an ink line of uniform thickness (*Fig. 8.39*). For heavier lines, different size pens are used. The stylus pen easily manages curves of short radius (*Fig. 8.42*). It is filled by means of an ink-stopper (*Fig. 8.40*) or other device and is used in a vertical position (*Fig. 8.41*). Acetate ellipse guides (*Fig. 8.43*) are used to draw mechanical ellipses or portions thereof in ink or pencil (*Figs. 8.44-8.45*). The guides are made in different sizes and different degrees of perspective.

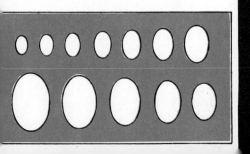

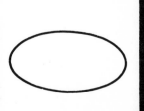

51

Fig. 8.46: Anna Marie Magagna.

TASTE WHY ENGLAND KNIGHTED BURNETT

SIR ROBERT BURNETT'S WHITE SATIN GIN

Fig. 8.47: Courtesy Sir Robert Burnett Co.

Fig. 8.48: Reese Brandt.

Fig. 8.49: Stonorov & Kahn, Architects, *Your Solar House*, **Simon & Schuster.**

Fig. 8.50: Irv Docktor.

Fig. 8.51: Eva Cellini., Courtesy of *The National Observer*

Because of the variety of tools that can be employed, the opacity of the ink and the fineness with which it can be controlled, ink is suited for precise mechanical drawing as well as loose freehand drawing. Varied ink techniques are aptly illustrated in Anna Marie Magagna's free flowing and expressive brush line drawing, Irv Docktor's textured realism and Reese Brandt's beautifully designed drawing, with its decorative pattern treatment.

9. Scratchboard

SCRATCHBOARD is essentially a medium to be used with ink. It is a specially surfaced (chalk coated) white board on which the drawing is done in ink, as required, and then the white areas and lines can be scratched or etched out with various tools. Because the ink lines do not spread on this surface, and the white lines are actually scratched out of it, extreme fineness and control of lines can be obtained.

Its reproduction qualities are magnificent; the drawings have a brilliant quality even in extreme reduction and on cheap news stock. It is a versatile medium, capable of crisp illustrations. It is economical because all the value range of a halftone is obtainable for the price of a line plate. It requires only ordinary drawing equipment. It can be corrected easily and unobtrusively. It can be done in color as well as black and white.

Techniques

The two major problems of technique in scratchboard, as in any other black-and-white medium, are the rendering of values and textures. In the following pages these techniques are carefully shown and applied in the illustrations. Scratchboard is most effective in reduced size, but for instruction purposes most illustrations are shown here at nearly working size as well as in reduction.

When drawing pen lines on scratchboard, do not use too much pressure (*Fig. 9.2*). Brush in

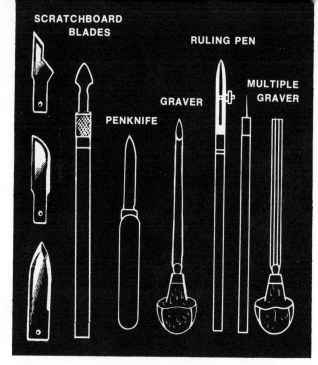

Fig. 9.1: Instruments Used for Scratchboard Drawing.

an area of the board with India ink (*Fig. 9.3*), putting it on smoothly and not too thickly. When the ink is thoroughly dry, scratch out white lines with a scratchboard tool (*Fig. 9.4*).

ROUGHS. Although certain corrections are easily made on scratchboard, any deeply scratched area is difficult to work over. The beginner is strongly advised to think and work out his problems carefully before attempting the finished drawing. Several pencil sketches can be made for composition and value or, in the case of a more complicated subject, a very careful pencil rendering can be made. In either case it is best for the less experienced to work only in tone and not try to simulate the scratchboard technique in the pencil-drawing stage. Next, the texture and value techniques can be experimented with on scratchboard by means of small "roughs" of various portions of the drawing.

Fig. 9.2.   Fig. 9.3.   Fig. 9.4.

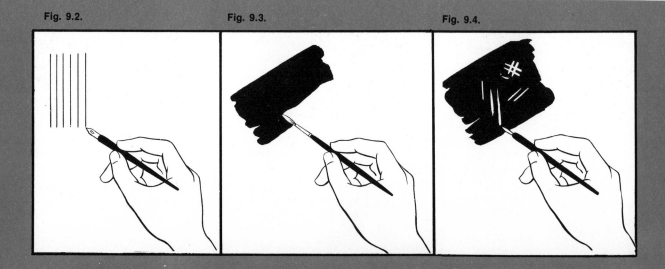

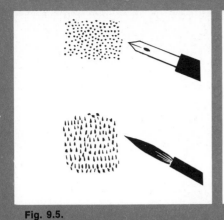
Fig. 9.5.

Fig. 9.6.

Fig. 9.7.

STIPPLE TECHNIQUE. Scratchboard can be drawn on directly with a pen or brush using stipple (*Fig. 9.5*) or line techniques similar to those described in the Pen and Ink chapter. For a stipple effect, apply solid black ink with a brush (*Fig. 9.6A*). Allow it to dry thoroughly, and then scratch out the white dots (*Fig. 9.6B*). A combination of black and white can be effected by first applying a solid area and stippling out with a pen (*Fig. 9.7A*), and then scratching out the white dots (*Fig. 9.7B*) to the top.

Fig. 9.8.

Fig. 9.9.

Fig. 9.10.

LINE TECHNIQUES. *Flat Tone*: Use a metal ruler or T-square as a guide for the blade when scratching out the white lines (*Fig. 9.8*). *Graded Tone*: Scratch out the whites, gradually increasing the width of the lines (*Fig. 9.9*). *Graded Tone, by Combination Method*: Ink in solid area and black pen lines (*Fig. 9.10A*), and then scratch out white lines (*Fig. 9.10B*).

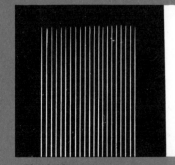
Fig. 9.11.

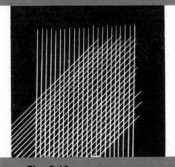
Fig. 9.12.

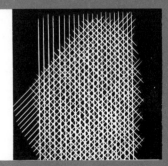
Fig. 9.13.

CROSS-HATCHING. Lines can be scratched across each other to give different value and pattern effects. (*Figs. 9.11-9.13*). Do not scratch too deeply or the scratchboard will chip. While all lines shown here are of the same thickness, it is possible to vary the thickness of the lines by using a penknife or wood engraving tool, as shown at the top of page 57.

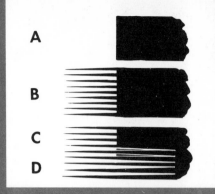

Fig. 9.14.

Fig. 9.15.

GRADED LINE TECHNIQUES. One method (*Fig. 9.14*) is to ink only half the area (A), draw graded lines to this area (B), scratch guide lines in black area (C), then scratch out between the lines (D). Another method (*Fig. 9.15*), is to ink the entire area (A), scratch out horizontal lines at the desired spacing (B), scratch out guide lines to points halfway between these horizontals (C), then scrape away black areas, leaving tapered lines (D).

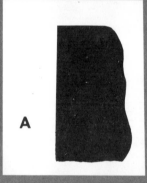

Fig. 9.16.

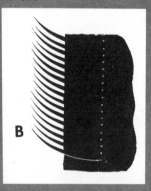

Fig. 9.17.

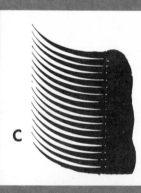

Fig. 9.18.

Figs. 9.16-9.18 show the application of the above procedure to curved lines, using a French curve.

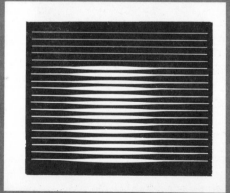

Fig. 9.19.

Fig. 9.20.

Shifting the width of the line gradually to another position (*Figs. 9.19-9.20*) enables the artist to control placements of lights and darks.

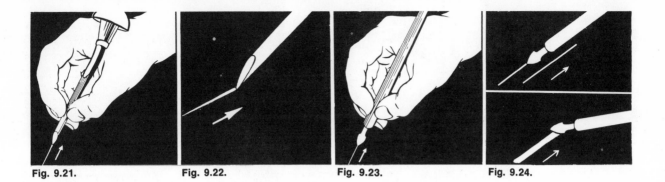

Fig. 9.21. Fig. 9.22. Fig. 9.23. Fig. 9.24.

USE OF THE GRAVER. The graver (used for wood engraving) is an excellent tool for scratching lines of varying width (*Figs. 9.21-9.22*). It can be used against a ruler or T-square for straight lines. The spoon-shaped scratchboard blade made by X-Acto can be used at the point for fine lines, and on the side for wide lines or areas (*Figs. 9.23-9.24*).

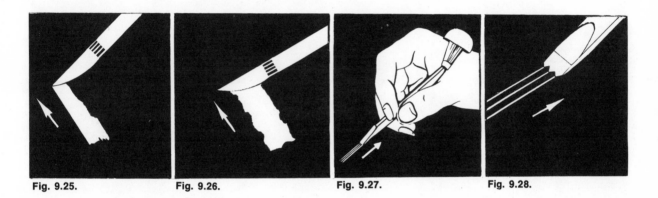

Fig. 9.25. Fig. 9.26. Fig. 9.27. Fig. 9.28.

Use the end of a curved X-Acto blade for scratching an area with one edge sharp, as in *Fig. 9.25*. Use the middle of a curved blade for scratching wide areas of white (*Fig. 9.26*). Strokes should overlap. The multiple-line graver will scratch two or more parallel lines at one stroke (*Figs. 9.27-9.28*).

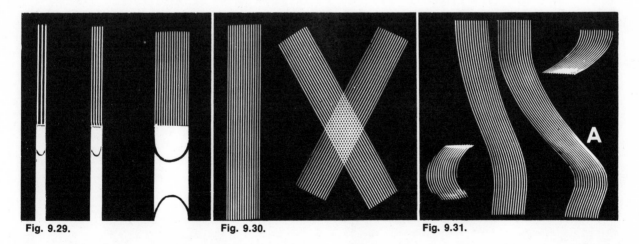

Fig. 9.29. Fig. 9.30. Fig. 9.31.

Effects achieved with multiple-line gravers of various widths are obtainable in fine or coarse screen sizes. Precise patterns are secured by crossing strokes. Do not cut too deeply.

Twisting the multiple graver during the stroke so that it is no longer parallel to the direction of the stroke produces a change in value (A). It is used for texture effects.

Fig. 9.33: Bell & Howell Co.

Fig. 9.35: Paul M. Breeden.

Fig. 9.32: Robert Greco, Stephen Goerl Assoc.

Fig. 9.34: Paul M. Breeden. *Defenders of Wildlife Magazine*

In these pages, specific working methods are shown for different types of illustrations and the appropriate techniques applied. Poor technique in scratchboard, as in other media, is indicated by weakness in reproduction, in lack of a good scale of values and a mixed or indefinite technique—the method of securing value and texture effects being incongruous in different parts of the illustration.

It is possible to do an entire drawing with only slight variation in line, but using pattern and texture differences, as in *Fig. 9.36*. This is particularly true of "stylized" and decorative drawings. Many scratchboard drawings have a mechanical stiffness that is the fault of the artist rather than the medium, because the medium is flexible. Styles can be as personal as in woodcuts and engravings, and much more easily obtained.

Fig. 9.36: H. Butt, S.W. Hobson, Ltd.

Fig. 9.37: Robert Greco, Stephen Goerl Assoc.

10. Shaded Line Media

EXAMINE THE DRAWINGS reproduced on this and the next page. You will notice that they appear to consist of black, white and a gray tone, which gradates from dark to light gray. Actually, the gray tones are an optical illusion, created by black dots of varying sizes. *Large* dots with small white spaces between them appear dark; *small* dots with larger white spaces appear light. This is essentially the same effect as was produced by pen and ink techniques, but now it is effected by a combination of paper with an embossed finish—raised dots—and varying pressure of a black drawing tool, usually litho pencil, litho crayon stick or very soft lead pencil. Another method of achieving simulated gray tones is through the use of "shading sheets," acetate sheets with an imprinted pattern.

The functions of these media are to expedite the drawing procedure and to produce some of the qualities or effects of continuous tone art at the cost and with the convenience of line printing procedures. This will be better understood when you read chapter 17 on Communications Media. It must be realized that, while adequate for the purposes for which they are designed, these media do not provide the tonal refinements of true continuous tone art.

Coquille and Glarco Boards

Coquille and Glarco boards are heavy drawing papers with embossed surfaces in various textures. By varying the pressure of the crayon or intensity of the drybrush, shading effects can be achieved, although one still has what amounts to a line reproduction drawing. Litho crayon, carbon, Conte, and chalk pencils can be used (*Fig. 10.1*). Ink can be applied with a brush or pen (*Fig. 10.2*), and poster white can be used over areas that have been drawn on to produce highlights or details (*Fig. 10.3*). This type of drawing paper is used primarily by cartoonists and fashion and merchandise illustrators for newspaper reproduction, although it can also be used for advertising and book illustration where halftone costs are prohibitive.

Fig. 10.1.

Fig. 10.2.

Fig. 10.3.

William Crawford, syndicated editorial cartoonist, does his illustrations on Coquille board, following the procedure illustrated herein. *Fig. 10.4* shows a sketch, with caption, which has been selected by the editor as the best of the sketches submitted for the day. (In this particular case, no changes were required.) The drawing was then worked up with a blue pencil directly on Coquille board. The blue pencil was used because it does not show in the reproduction, though it may remain in the completed art. Since the actual reproduction of the cartoon in the newspaper was 7" x 9", the original was drawn about twice that size. After the pencil work, the inking was done in a drybrush technique (*Fig. 10.5*). Finally, the gray tones were drawn with a litho crayon #3, and a few lines accented with jet black pencil. *Fig. 10.6* shows the completed cartoon as it appeared in the paper.

The political cartoonist must of necessity work rapidly and produce a drawing that is clearly and easily understood with a minimum of caption. Mr. Crawford does this with a very definite style which is quite forceful and highly individual.

Fig. 10.6: William Crawford, *Newark Evening News.*

Fig. 10.7A: The Ink Drawing.

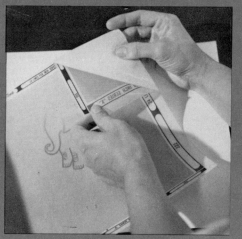

Fig. 10.7B: A Shading Sheet.

Fig. 10.7C: Cutting Shading Sheet.

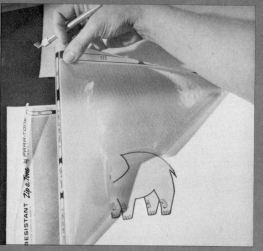

Fig. 10.7D: Removing Excess Pattern.

Fig. 10.7E: The Finished Drawing.

Shading and Pattern Sheets

Using transparent acetate shading sheets with an imprinted pattern is a valuable time-saver to the artist, as well as a means for obtaining graphic effects which would otherwise be difficult or impossible. Through use of these shading sheets, varied tones and patterns can be applied to a drawing. For its most common application, a pen and ink drawing is done in outline and solid blacks on drawing paper or board (*Fig. 10.7A*); the shading sheet is then applied to areas of the original drawing (*Fig. 10.7B)* where a tone or texture is desired. It is now cut to the required shape (*Fig. 10.7C)*, and the excess pattern removed *(Fig. 10.7D)*. For complete adherence it should then be burnished, preferably with a protective sheet of tracing paper over the pattern area.

Types of Shading Sheets

There are four major types of shading sheets: (1) A shading sheet made with the pattern printed on the top and the underside coated with a transparent adhesive. This allows the sheet to be placed over a drawing, pressed down and the excess cut away or smaller pattern areas scratched off. A fixative can be sprayed over the pattern to protect it after all artwork has been completed. (2) A second, more useful type has the pattern printed on the underside of the shading sheet so that it is protected by the clear acetate above. An adhesive on the back of the sheet consists of wax or clear cement. (3) A third type has no adhesive and is useful when one wishes merely to lay the shading sheet over the drawing. (4) The fourth type is an acetate shading film from which the pattern can be transferred to the surface and area desired by rubbing with a stylus.

Shading sheets are made with a black pattern for use on a white or light colored ground and with a white pattern for use on a dark or black ground. The patterns available are lines, dots and textures, either abstract or representing bricks, water, wood, symbols or pictograms (*Fig. 10.14*).

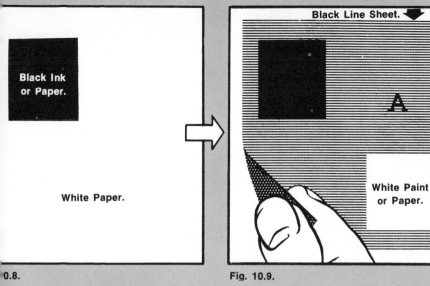

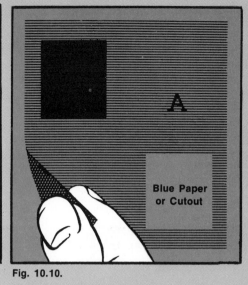

Fig. 10.8. Fig. 10.9. Fig. 10.10.

BLACK PATTERN SHEETS. If on a sheet of white drawing paper (*Fig 10.8*) we fill in a small area with black ink, then place over the paper a black pattern sheet (*Fig. 10.9*), we note that the pattern lines do not show over the small black area. Wherever we wish an area of white we can either cut out and remove the pattern sheet, or paste a piece of white paper over the area, or paint it out with white poster paint.

If we place the pattern sheet over blue or other colored paper with a black area (*Fig. 10.10*), we note that the black lines show on the blue ground but not on the black. If we cut out the pattern, the colored ground will show.

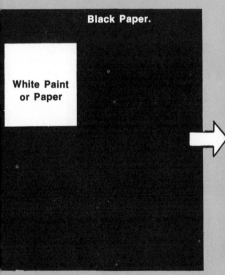

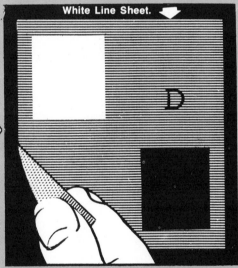

Fig. 10.11. Fig. 10.12. Fig. 10.13.

WHITE PATTERN SHEETS. However, the white pattern sheet shows on a black ground (*Figs. 10.11* and *10.12*) and disappears over the white area. It can be cut away to reveal the black ground. To obtain solid white either paint or paper can be used.

Placed over a blue ground, the pattern sheet shows white lines on blue (*Fig. 10.13*).

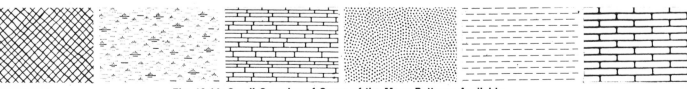

Fig. 10.14: Small Samples of Some of the Many Patterns Available.

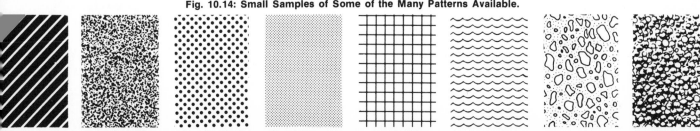

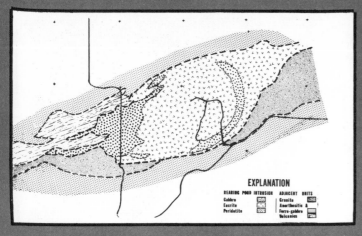

Fig. 10.15: James Olmstead.

Fig. 10.16:

EXAMPLES OF SHADING SHEET APPLICATIONS

Fig. 10.17: Dave Dewhurst, Art Students League.

Fig. 10.18.

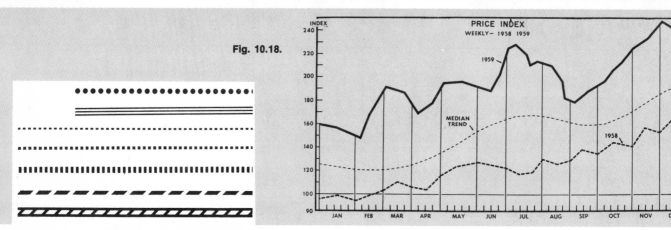

Line and Pattern Tapes

A wide variety of patterns and lines, in black and white and color, transparent and opaque, are obtainable in plastic tape form with adhesive backing, in a wide selection of widths from 1/64th of an inch to ½ inch, and over 25 yards long. These are very useful for graphs, chartmaking, maps, borders, dotted and dash lines, etc. (*Fig. 10.18*). They are useful for both print and nonprint applications. For use, the tape is positioned (*Fig. 10.19*), cut off at the ends (*Fig. 10.20*), and the excess removed. The tape should be burnished down for firm adherence. Some tapes are packaged in a dispenser case (*Fig. 10.21*), which is useful for storage and easier application.

Fig. 10.19.

Fig. 10.20.

Fig. 10.21.

11. Color Aids

RELATED, application-wise, to the shading sheets are color overlay acetate sheets and colored paper aids.

Colored Paper

Colored papers are of several types: those colored in manufacture with dyes which impregnate the paper throughout; white papers printed on one side with printing ink; and white papers silkscreen printed with a uniform, opaque coating of oil-based pigment. The better papers, especially the latter type, are color coded for matching and are available in a wide variety of beautiful colors in many tints, shades, warm and cool grays, black and white. Colored papers serve both as background support and for cutouts of areas, shapes and subject matter. They accept paint, ink and transfer materials such as lettering and patterns. They are great time-savers and are very convenient because of their great variety, flexibility and precolored aspect. Colored paper aids are equally suitable for print reproduction, displays, presentations, television art, packaging and decorative design.

PROCEDURE

The illustration shown in *Fig. 11.4A* was designed for filmstrip reproduction; it is one of many "frames" used in the series. After a preliminary color sketch, an accurate outline drawing was made on tracing paper. This, like all the art in the series, was done in the same size as had been planned for the finished art that was to be photographed with color film. The various shapes used were designed to accommodate the size and amount of lettering required. The shapes were traced onto their corresponding colored papers, cut out with razor blade or scissors (*Fig. 11.1*), and the edges smoothed with sandpaper where necessary (*Fig. 11.2*). The top black panel was roughly torn along a folded edge. Each of these units was rubber-cemented into position on the background paper, using the tracing as a guide for positioning (*Fig. 11.3*); then the transfer lettering (see page 83) was applied. Since this is not reproduced here in the colors used in the original art, the color effectiveness is lost.

Fig. 11.1.

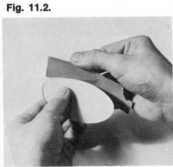

Fig. 11.2.

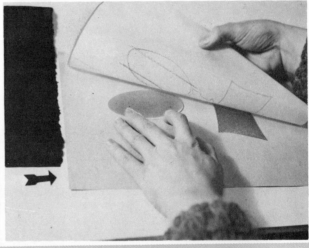

Fig. 11.3.

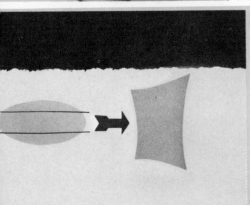

Fig. 11.4: Paper Units in Place Before Lettering.

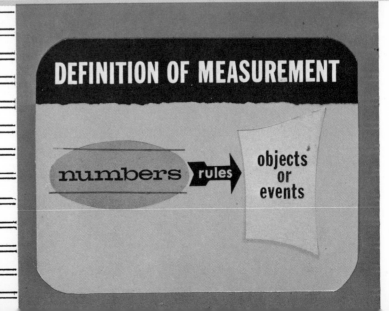

Fig. 11.4A: The Completed Filmstrip Frame.

DEFINITION OF MEASUREMENT

numbers rules objects or events

Color Overlay Sheets

Color overlay sheets are made of acetate and are printed in either transparent or opaque flat color, with a glossy or matte finish. They are available with or without adhesive backing, depending upon the application. The sheet, or a portion of it, is placed over a drawing. On some types, the color can be scratched or scraped off with a plastic stylus or removed with a solvent, where the color is not desired in the drawing. On others it is merely cut out and removed. Another type permits transfer of the color to the drawing by rubbing, somewhat like transfer lettering. Transparent color overlays can be used directly to make overhead transparencies for projection, as well as artwork for presentations, displays, television and printing.

Color acetate sheets of transparent red or orange are used to make color separation overlays. They can be photocopied as line art for platemaking. Such overlays can also be used for photo-silkscreen art preparation. They are obtainable with varied working characteristics as described above. Color separation procedures are shown on page 107.

Techniques and Materials

The series of illustrations on this page shows the procedure for making a color visual, using a pressure adhering color overlay sheet, transfer lettering and transfer symbols (arrows); the visual was prepared in this particular instance for copying on 35 mm color film for slide projection. For print preparation, it would be more economical to prepare this as a color separation mechanical.

Since a gray background was decided upon, gray TV illustration board was selected as the base and cut to 11" x 14", allowing an adequate border for the 6" x 8" drawing area. A white silhouette map of China was required, so a white paper cutout was made, as this is easier to work on than a white painted area. Since a color area was required within the map, an acetate sheet of transparent color overlay with adhesive backing was decided upon. The arrows were provided by a transfer sheet, as was the lettering. (The latter materials are described in the chapter on Lettering and Type, page 78.)

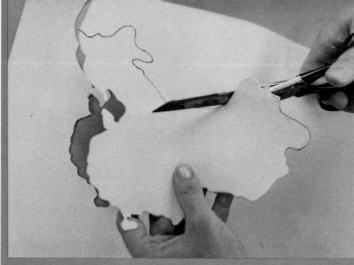

Fig. 11.5.

1. With sharp scissors the map is carefully cut out of the white paper, following the outline previously drawn on it (*Fig. 11.5*).

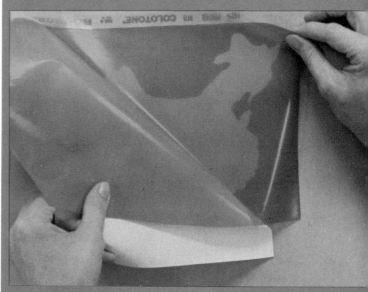

Fig. 11.8.

4. The acetate transparent color sheet is placed over the white cutout map area, slowly peeled away from its backing sheet (*Fig. 11.8*) and then gently rubbed down on the map, care being taken to avoid wrinkles.

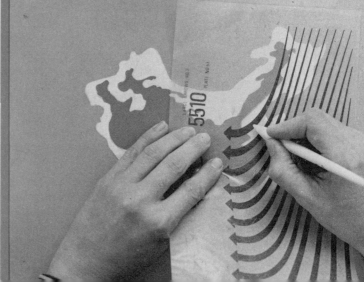

Fig. 11.11.

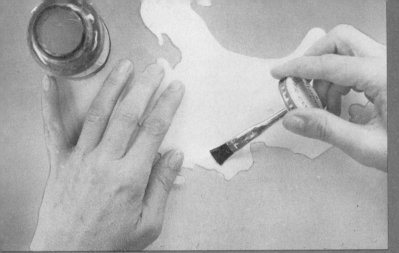

Fig. 11.6.

2. Rubber cement is applied to the back of the paper cutout, which is then turned over and adhered to the gray board while still wet (*Fig. 11.6*).

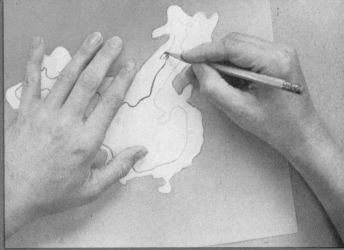

Fig. 11.7.

3. The outline of the mountain area is transferred to the map from a sheet of tracing paper, on which it had been drawn previously (*Fig. 11.7*).

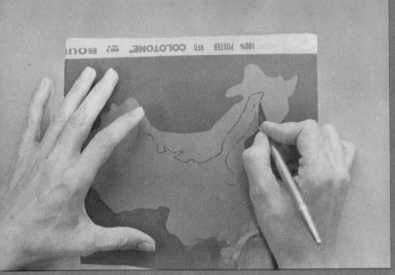

Fig. 11.9.

5. The mountain area outline, which is visible through the color sheet, is cut out with a frisket knife, care being taken to cut only through the acetate overlay and not the paper (*Fig. 11.9*).

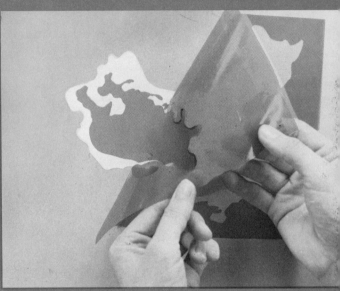

Fig. 11.10.

6. The excess color sheet area is peeled away from the map, leaving the mountain area intact (*Fig. 11.10*).

7. The arrows and the lettering are transferred into position (*Figs. 11.11-11.13*).

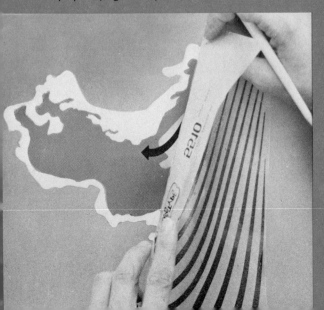

MOUNTAIN AREAS

Fig. 11.12.

Fig. 11.13: The Completed Film Slide·

12. Photography

AN UNDERSTANDING of photographic procedures is of definite importance to the commercial artist for several reasons: photography can be used directly as a subject or action information source for illustration; much photographic material is handled and utilized by the artist in design, layout and production functions; most artwork and type have to be photographically copied for printing or for nonprint use.

The mechanical aspects of photography involve the following: the selection of a camera that will do the job required; knowledge and skill in the operation or use of the camera; selection and use of proper film; processing of that film and photoprinting. A brief examination of each of the aspects mentioned will be helpful in understanding the rudiments of photography.

Types of Cameras

A camera is essentially a box with a lens at one end which allows a light image to enter and be focused on sensitized film at the other end (*Fig. 12.1*). A "shutter" controls the *duration* of the exposure, and a "diaphram" controls the lens *opening*—the area of lens used according to the setting decided upon for that particular exposure. On the basis of their structure and the manner in which they function, cameras can be classified into three basic categories: the simple *fixed focus* camera, with a "finder" through which one looks to approximate the scene or area that will register on the film; the *view* camera (*Figs. 12.2-12.3*), a focusing camera in which the image travels directly from the lens to the ground glass viewing area, where it can be seen in the same size as it will register on the film, which is placed in the position of the ground glass when the exposure is made; and the *reflex* camera (*Figs. 12.4-12.5*), a focusing camera in which the image travels through the lens to a mirror, from which it is deflected to a ground glass for viewing while the film remains in place in the camera.

FIXED FOCUS CAMERAS. Simple fixed focus cameras are not very versatile in terms of speed of exposure or varied light conditions. They are not capable of taking "close-ups" and do not take pictures which are capable of much enlargement, as the negatives are not very sharp. Most models do have "flash" capability. Film is of roll or cartridge type, from postage stamp size to 620-size negative.

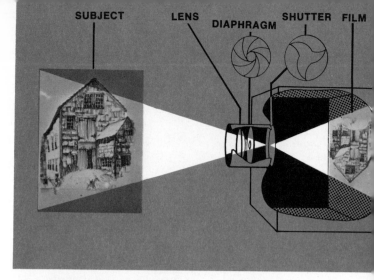

SUBJECT   LENS   DIAPHRAGM   SHUTTER   FILM

Fig. 12.1: Principle of the Camera.

Fig. 12.2: A View Camera.

Fig. 12.3: A Studio (View) Camera in Use.

Fig. 12.4: The Single Lense Reflex Camera.

Fig. 12.5: The Twin Lens Reflex Camera.

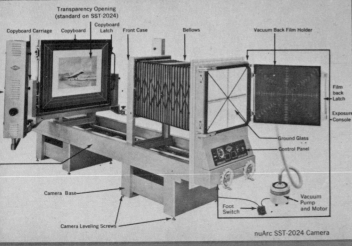

Fig. 12.6: A Horizontal Copy Camera.

VIEW CAMERAS. View cameras range from 2¼" x 3¼" negative size to 11" x 14" negative size, all in sheet form, though some cameras utilize roll film adapters. Most view cameras have lens boards and film backs with vertical, horizontal, tilting and shifting action, and revolving backs, which allow for perspective or distortion control as well as greater image positioning flexibility. Since they generally have to be used with a tripod, they are not as useful for action and candid photography as are the small reflex cameras.

REFLEX CAMERAS. There are two types of reflex cameras, the *single lens* reflex (SLR) (*Fig. 12.4*), in which the mirror moves out of the way at the instant of exposure of the image to the film; and the *twin lens* reflex (TLR) (*Fig. 12.5*), which has one lens for viewing the mirror-deflected image and another lens through which the image travels to the film at the same time, thus allowing the image to be viewed even during exposure. Most twin lens reflex cameras use roll film that gives a 2¼" x 2¼" size negative. Most single lens reflex cameras use 35 mm roll film, though some use 2¼" x 2¼" size and some use larger sizes, in sheet film form. The 33 mm single lens reflex is probably the most convenient camera to carry and use, especially for color slides, but larger film sizes have to be employed for certain applications and uses.

Camera Use

Two separate aspects of camera use should be considered: *picture-taking* of actual objects or activities, and *copying* of other photos, art, type, etc. Picture-taking is generally done with a small camera that can be hand held or used on a tripod; copying is generally done with a large camera, similar to a view camera, placed in permanent or semi-permanent position in a photo-work area or darkroom. Small cameras used for picture-taking can also be used for copy work of certain types. However, copy films for platemaking for printing are made same size as the final printed material, so true copy cameras (*Fig. 12.6*) must be capable of handling large film, up to an average of 20" x 24", and also possess other operating features that picture-taking cameras do not require. For picture-taking, roll films are now generally used, but small-size sheet film, up to 8" x 10", is also used commercially, both in continuous tone black and white and in color. High contrast films known as "litho" films are used for the printing arts. These are also used to achieve many of the experimental and "creative" photographic effects shown on page 75.

Picture-Taking and Printing

Fig. 12.7A: Film Negative.

Photographic film is coated with an emulsion containing a chemical, silver chloride, that is sensitive to light. When this film is developed the silver particles that have been exposed to light are converted to dark silver particles, creating a negative image on the film (*Fig. 12.7A*); the term "negative" refers to the fact that what was *light* in the original subject registers *dark* on the film. In order to obtain a positive image (one that represents the lights and darks as they appear in the original subject), this negative is exposed by means of light to another sensitized film or to sensitized paper and chemically developed, resulting correspondingly in either a positive film transparency or a paper photoprint (*Fig. 12.7B*). If the positive is made by direct physical contact with the negative, the image on the transparency or print will be the *same size* as on the negative and is called a contact print. If it is made in an enlarger (a kind of camera in reverse) by projecting light through the negative and through a lens onto film or paper, the image will be larger than on the negative and is called, naturally, an enlargement.

From a technical point of view, a "normal" photograph is one which combines a good range of values in the gray scale with some definitely black tones and white highlights. There should be good detail in the dark areas as well as in the light ones. A photograph that has too much contrast and lacks sufficient gray tones may be blocked up in the dark areas and washed out in the light ones (*Fig. 12.8*). A "flat" print, on the other hand, has an overall gray cast, without any good darks or lights (*Fig. 12.9*). Of course, these faults may have their origin in the negatives; but compensation can be made in the print or enlargement by using a grade of photographic paper which will tend to correct the fault. A soft grade of paper will soften the effects of an over-contrasty negative, and a hard paper will accentuate the values of a soft negative. Thus you can order the type of print necessary for the effect you wish, or you may even direct the platemaker to effect such a change in the platemaking stage if you already have the print and cannot have a new one made. Alterations can also be made by retouching the negative or print. (See page 76.)

Fig. 12.7B: Photo Print, Normal Contrast.

Fig. 12.8: High Contrast.

Fig. 12.9: Low Contrast.

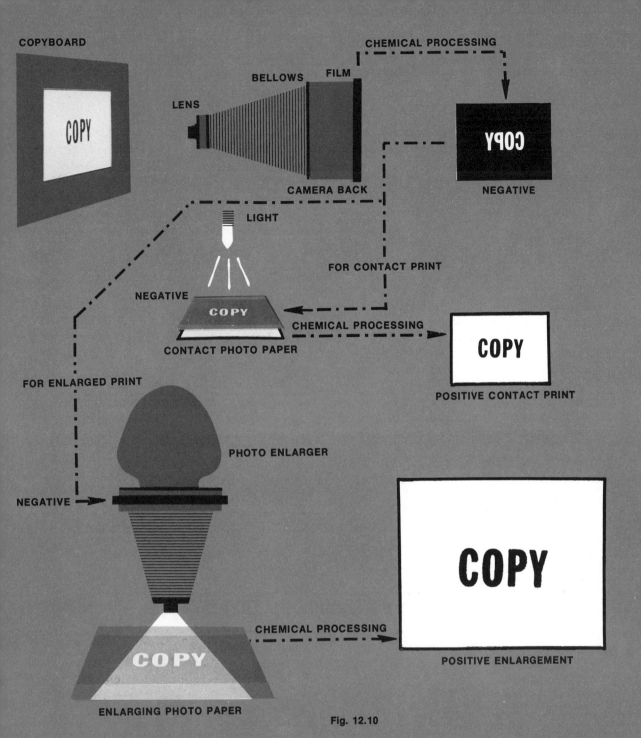

COPYBOARD

LENS

BELLOWS

FILM

CHEMICAL PROCESSING

CAMERA BACK

NEGATIVE

LIGHT

FOR CONTACT PRINT

NEGATIVE

CHEMICAL PROCESSING

CONTACT PHOTO PAPER

COPY

POSITIVE CONTACT PRINT

FOR ENLARGED PRINT

PHOTO ENLARGER

NEGATIVE

CHEMICAL PROCESSING

COPY

POSITIVE ENLARGEMENT

COPY

ENLARGING PHOTO PAPER

Fig. 12.10

Fig. 12.10 gives an overview of the negative-positive relationship in photography, the sequence of procedures, and the difference between contact printing and enlarging. Here, the material to be photocopied—indicated by the word "copy"—is placed on the copyboard. The "copy" may be an illustration, a photographic print or type proofs. If this were a picture-taking procedure, a scene, a still-life or people would replace the copyboard; but all further steps would be the same. We have shown the original copy and the negative image to be the *same* size. However, the image could have been made *larger* on the negative by moving the copyboard closer to the film in the camera back and *extending* the bellows to increase the *distance between the film and the*

lens to keep the image in focus. To make the negative image *smaller* than the art, the reverse would be done; the copyboard would be moved further from the film in the camera, and the bellows would be *shortened*, moving the lens closer to the film. After exposure in the camera the film is processed and becomes a negative. This negative can be used to make a same size positive print (contact) or an enlarged print. Thus we note that there are two stages at which the image size can be manipulated; in the picture-taking or copy stage, where size is limited by the size of the camera film holder, and again in the print enlarging stage, where size is almost unlimited. Photostats would be made the same way, but using *photopaper* instead of film for the negative stage.

Color Photography

Color photographic images exist in two forms: as transparencies and as prints. Both forms originate as negatives. You do not obtain color negatives from *reversal* film (film indicated by the word "chrome": Koda*chrome*, Ekta*chrome*, Ansco*chrome*, etc.) because during the processing such film is reversed into a positive, which is the film or slide you receive. This film or slide is known as a *transparency*.

On the other hand, if you use Koda*color* or Ansco*color*, a color negative will be obtained upon processing the film, and from the color negative you can obtain either a color paper print or a transparency, or both. It is possible to get a color print from a Kodachrome transparency, but an intermediate negative has to be made; a print can then be made from the negative, although there is some loss in color quality as compared with a print made directly from a Kodacolor negative. It is also possible to obtain a type of color print known as a *dye transfer* from a Kodachrome transparency. To do so, three separate film positives, each representing one of the primary colors, are dyed, and the images transferred, in register, to a sheet of dye transfer paper. Such prints are of excellent color quality and sharpness, but are expensive.

Most printing press reproductions are made from positive color transparencies, but they can be made from dye transfers and other color prints. Paper prints are known as *reflection* copy. Color corrections and changes can be made by means of filters in photoprinting, by means of dyes applied directly on the transparency or print and by means of other procedures such as bleaching. Extensive opaque color retouching, using airbrushing for example, can be done on color prints.

Fig. 12.11

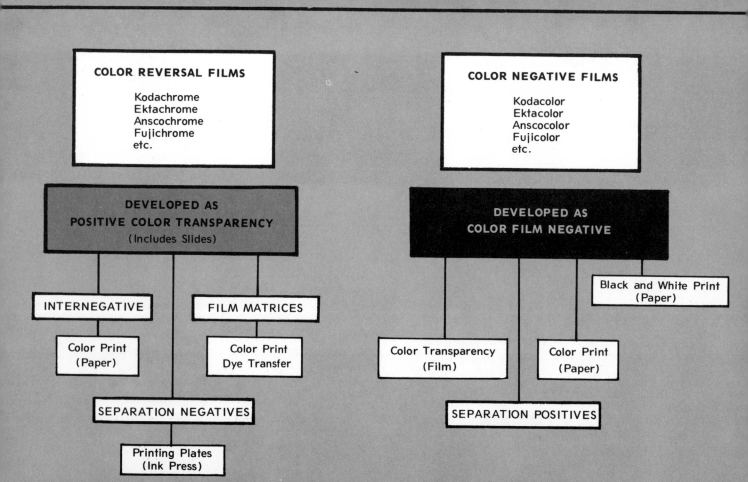

COLOR PHOTOGRAPHY
TYPES OF FILMS AND PRINTS

COLOR REVERSAL FILMS

Kodachrome
Ektachrome
Anscochrome
Fujichrome
etc.

COLOR NEGATIVE FILMS

Kodacolor
Ektacolor
Anscocolor
Fujicolor
etc.

DEVELOPED AS POSITIVE COLOR TRANSPARENCY
(Includes Slides)

DEVELOPED AS COLOR FILM NEGATIVE

INTERNEGATIVE

FILM MATRICES

Black and White Print
(Paper)

Color Print
(Paper)

Color Print
Dye Transfer

Color Transparency
(Film)

Color Print
(Paper)

SEPARATION NEGATIVES

SEPARATION POSITIVES

Printing Plates
(Ink Press)

Special Effects

While the layman thinks of photography as a literal medium, it is capable of highly personal interpretation and much variation. Witness some of the highly creative fashion, editorial, illustrative and advertising photographs. These serve to convey impressions or emotions and illustrate points much more effectively than "straight" photographs possibly could.

HIGH AND LOW KEY PHOTOS. High and low key photographs are deviations from a normal photograph mainly in the matter of lighting. The high key photo consists mostly of values in the higher, or lighter, end of the value scale, but with enough highlights and dark accents to avoid being a flat print. It has an airy, dainty quality that makes it quite appropriate for feminine fashion, cosmetics, baby subjects and imaginative themes. The low key photo makes use of the low or dark end of the scale. It is suitable for highly dramatic effects, for strong, masculine subjects and somber themes.

NEGATIVE IMAGE PRINTS. A negative image print can be very effective, as in the cover illustration (*Fig. 12.12*). This is obtained by making a positive image on film, instead of paper, then making from this a negative image print by contact or enlargement.

DISTORTION. Distortion of subject matter is effective at times. With a view camera distortion can be obtained directly on the negative by tilting the camera's ground glass until the desired effect is obtained. Distortion can also be controlled when enlarging by tilting the negative holder and the enlarging paper during exposure. Also, certain camera lenses, such as the "fish eye" lens, produce image distortion.

SOLARIZATION. Solarization is achieved by briefly exposing the negative or print to light during development, then completing the development in the usual manner. Depending upon the extent and manner of exposing, this results in a modified or complete outline form, possibly combined with black and white areas which have some of the characteristics of a negative and some of a positive (*Fig. 12.13*).

MONTAGES AND COMPOSITES. A montage is the combination of two or more different images on the same print (*Fig. 17.6*, page 111), usually managed in the enlarging or other photoprinting process. A *composite* is an

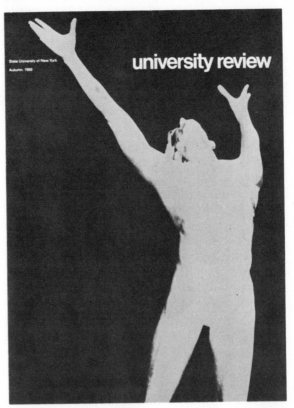

Fig. 12.12: Negative Print.
Hermann Bachmann, State University of New York.

Fig. 12.13: Partially Solarized Print. Ernest Beadle,
Douglas D. Simon Agency.

assemblage of individual photographs, usually pasted in a desired arrangement and photocopied or printed. In a montage, images merge and overlap at their edges, while in a composite sharp divisions are characteristic. Montages serve to combine different images which could not be physically photographed together, though for certain subjects the same effect could be obtained by controlled double or multiple exposure on the same negative (*Fig. 12.15*).

PHOTOGRAMS. A photogram (*Fig. 12.16*) is a photographic print made without the use of a camera, strange as it may seem. In the simplest form of making a photogram, an opaque or semi-opaque object is placed on a sheet of photographic paper in the darkroom and exposed to a brief flash of light. The paper then is developed in the usual manner, resulting in a negative image formed by the light reaching the paper directly and through the object. If the object is opaque, for example a fern leaf, a white silhouette of the fern on a black background will result. By shifting objects around and making multiple exposures on the same paper, many interesting and often unpredictable results will be obtained.

HIGH CONTRAST PRINTS. High contrast prints (*Fig. 12.18*), much used in illustrative and advertising photography, are generally achieved by copying a normal photograph on high contrast film such as Kodalith or Cronalith, then making a high contrast positive contact print or enlargement from the negative. This drops out most of the intermediate tones and accentuates the dark image areas or details, giving almost the effect of a drawing.

POSTERIZATION. Posterization (*Fig. 12.19*) really is an elaboration of high contrast photography. Instead of one high contrast copy negative, at least two or three are made; in the latter case one negative registers the lightest areas of the image, the second is exposed and developed for the intermediate tones and the third registers only the darkest tones of the image. Through multiple printing the negatives result in the two- or three-tone image.

TEXTURES AND PATTERNS. Texture or pattern effects on photographs (*Fig. 12.17*) can be obtained by placing a specially made texture screen over the paper during all or part of the exposure step when enlarging. Texture screens simulate etching effects, canvas and other patterns. Texture effects can also be incorporated in a negative image when photocopying a photograph or illustration for platemaking.

Fig. 12.14: **Montage. Morecraft and Oliwa**

Fig. 12.15: **Multiple Exposure. William Oliwa**

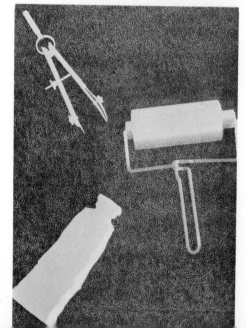

Fig. 12.16: **Photogram. Student, BOCES.**

Fig. 12.17: Texture Screens ⬇ ⬆ ➡

Fig. 12.19: Posterization. Courtesy Eastman Kodak Co.

Fig. 12.18: High Contrast Print.
I. J. Mittleman

Retouching

Photo retouching can be done on either the film negative or the positive print, but in commercial work it is most often done on the latter. Retouching can be anything from a few simple darks and highlights added with a sable brush and retouch grays to complete coverage of the photograph by airbrushing. The negative is usually worked on in portrait, and often fashion, retouching. Where lightening of portions of the positive print without loss of detail or texture is required, this is best done on the negative, if available and if large enough to work on.

Retouching on a print is done for several reasons: (1) To insure good reproduction when printed in a newspaper, magazine or other media; (2) to "slick up" the product for advertising or other purposes so that its good points are accented and it is shown to its best possible advantage; (3) to make corrections or alterations in the subject; and (4) to adapt the photograph to certain effects or shapes governed by the layout or design or by the combining of artwork and photography. A retouched print is reproduced in the same manner as an unretouched print.

Handling and Mounting

Photographs should be handled carefully to avoid cracking the emulsion and should not be written on with anything that will cause indentation on the print, as this will either show in reproduction or make it difficult for the retoucher if the print is to be airbrushed. When necessary to mark for size or write on the print, do so with a China marking or audiovisual pencil. Such marks can easily be removed by rubbing with cotton dipped in talcum powder. Whenever possible, do your writing on a tracing paper overlay and attach it to the photograph.

Permanent mounting of prints is best done with dry mounting tissue, which requires the use of an electric iron or, better yet, a dry mounting press. Rubber cement can be used—both the back of the print and the mounting board should be coated—and the rubber cement allowed to dry before placing the print on the mount. For temporary mounting use the rubber cement on one surface only and adhere while still wet. Rubber cement stains with age, affecting the print in later years.

Fig. 12.21. Original Photo

Fig. 12.22. Retouched Photo, Ray Crouch

13. Computer Art

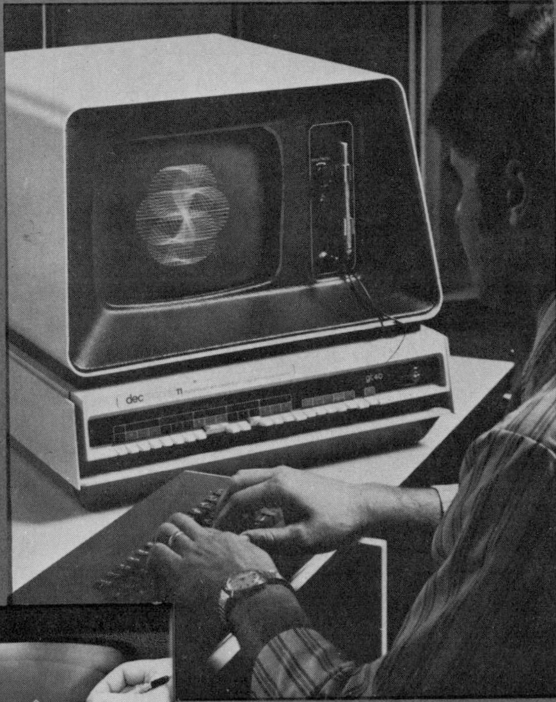

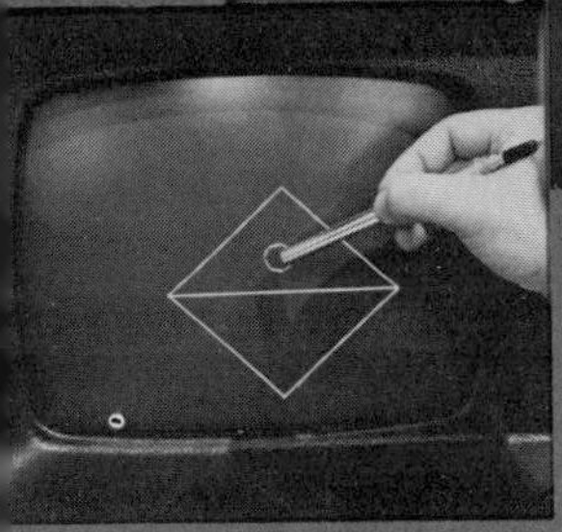

A COMPUTER is a machine that processes data; it manipulates information to arrive at a conclusion, to facilitate a decision or simply to record a fact. It consists of several units: an *input* device through which it is fed information; a *control* device, which we might compare to a traffic cop's functions; a *storage* unit, for retaining the information fed to it; a *central processing* unit, for performing the arithmetic and comparison functions; and an *output* device, which delivers the end product, which might be typewritten material, punched paper tape with coded information, an image or a drawing on paper. The output device may be a cathode ray tube on which type characters or drawn images are displayed (*Fig. 13.1*), a drawing device known as a plotter (*Fig. 13.2*), which the computer controls to draw images on paper with a stylus pen, or any of a number of other mechanisms.

The computer graphics system is particularly useful in displaying dynamic, fast changing information. Drawings can be instantly modified by the designer by using a "light pen"—an electronic device—directly on the drawing or diagram displayed on the cathode ray display tube (*Fig. 13.1*).

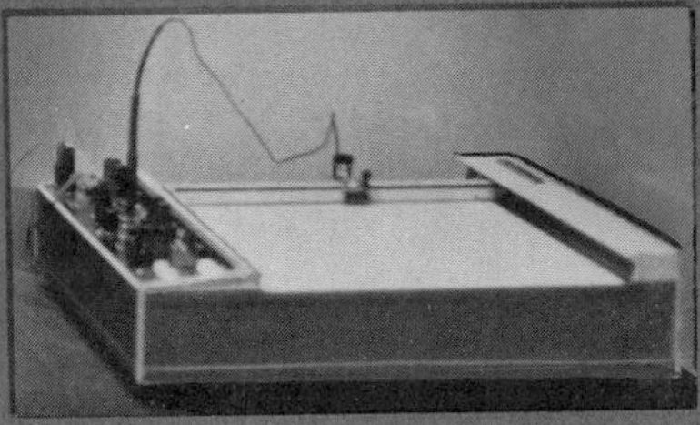

Uses of Computer Art

A computer can be programmed to perform such diverse art functions as showing different perspective views of a contemplated house design (*Fig. 13.3*) and altering these images to conform to changed specifications by the designer. It can draw the human form in different positions (*Fig. 13.4*); this is useful, for example, in determining measurements for instrument or control locations for airplane cockpit design. It can plot terrain configurations and perform innumerable other art and design functions. It has even been used to make animated motion picture films.

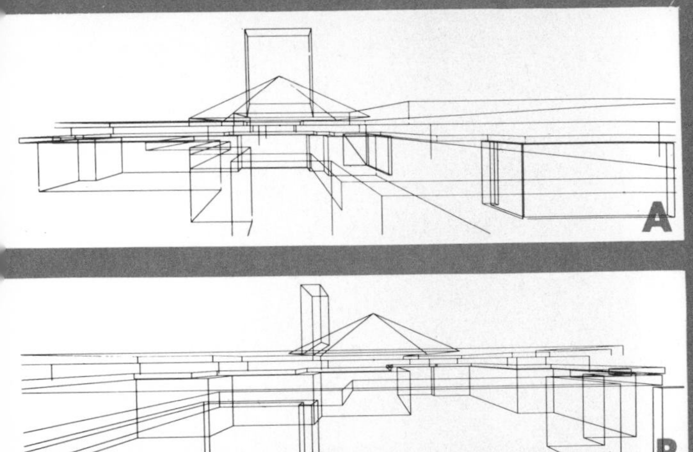

Fig. 13.1: Computer Image, Cathode Ray Tube, Digital Equipment Corp.

Fig. 13.1A: Using Light Pen.

Fig. 13.2: A Plotter.

Fig. 13.3: A and B: Stages of Computer Drawn Perspective; C: Rendering Based on Computer Plot. A. Bernholtz and E. Bierstone

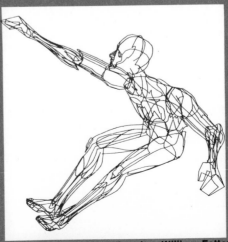

Fig. 13.4: Computer Drawing. William Fetter, Computer Graphics, Boeing Co.

14. Lettering and Typography

REPRESENTATIONS of the alphabet are generally termed "lettering" when hand drawn (*Fig. 14.1*), and "type" when impressions are printed from stock letter forms of metal or wood (*Fig. 14.2*) or are photographically produced from type images on film. Each of these two general categories can be further broken down.

Hand Lettering

Hand lettering is prepared both for direct reading and for reproduction. It can be done rather sketchily for the preliminary stage of a design or an advertisement or editorial layout. In which case it is known as "rough" or "layout" lettering (*Fig. 14.3*). It can be done in a more refined version for comprehensives and presentations in which stage it is known as "comp" lettering (*Fig. 14.4*). The final form of the hand drawn lettering for reproduction or direct use is known as "finished" lettering (*Fig. 14.5*). Rough and comp lettering may also be done as an indication of lettering that is to be eventually typeset rather than hand drawn.

Type

There are two broad classifications of type: *hot* type, which is the traditional, universal method of inking a relief letter of metal or wood and printing its impression on paper; and *cold* type, which is produced either photographically from an image on film or by a "strike on" method wherein a typewriterlike machine with relief characters makes type images by striking a carbon coated plastic ribbon. The essential functional differences between hot and cold type are that the former method requires ink, duplicate type letters and a press to form the letter images, while the latter requires only one set of letters of any typeface and no printer's ink or press. There are other important differences, but the ones mentioned are identifying characteristics.

HOT TYPE:. *Letterpress.* Metal relief type can be set by hand (*Fig. 14.6*), but is usually set by machine, such as Linotype (*Fig. 14.7*), then inked, and the image transferred to paper by a hand operated or motorized press (*Fig. 14.8*). Type may be set for direct printing by letterpress or reproduction proofs made for printing by offset. The size range of type is from 4 points to 4 inches high; type of the latter size is usually of wood. Letterpress is the most universal typesetting method, but is now losing ground to cold type, primarily phototypesetting.

Fig. 14.1: Lettering.

Fig. 14.2: Type.

Fig. 14.3: "Rough" or Layout Lettering.

Fig. 14.4: "Comp" Lettering.

Fig. 14.5: Finished Lettering.

Fig. 14.6: Handset Type.

Fig. 14.7: Linotype Machine.

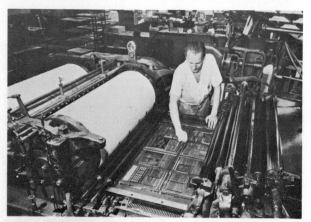

Fig. 14.8: Press.

COLD TYPE:. *Phototypesetting and photolettering*. There are many letter imaging systems based on the photographic exposure of individual letter forms from a film negative onto photographic paper or film which is then developed automatically or manually. There are two major systems: those imaging letters by contact (*Fig. 14.9*), providing only the same size as on the negative; and those imaging letters by projection, providing the same size as well as reduced or enlarged letters from the same negative. Display sizes up to 3½ inches, text sizes and combination sizes are available in systems ranging from simple manual to complex computerized units, now an important source for reproduction type.

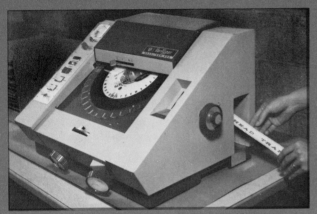

Fig. 14.9: Headliner Photo Display Type Machine.

COLD TYPE:. *Strike-on or direct image*. Machines which operate on the principle of the typewriter, but with proportional letters and unit spacing capability, are known as "strike-on" or direct impression composers (*Fig. 14.10*). These machines which range from manual to computer-operated systems, for direct use and print and nonprint applications, can justify type and usually can interchange typefaces. Size range (see page 91) is from 6 points to 14 points, suitable for text and small headline copy. Using this method, business forms can be ruled and lettered inexpensively for reproduction.

Fig. 14.10: Strike-on Type Machine, the IBM Selectric Composer.

Other Lettering Methods

The artist has other means of utilizing or making lettering such as the *transfer* and *template* methods, which do not fit specifically into the categories of type and hand lettering mentioned, but which, in most cases, are related to one or more of them.

PREFABRICATED LETTERS. This category includes preprinted two-dimensional letters merely requiring adherence or transfer to the surface on which they are to be used (*Fig. 14.11*). Though primarily for headline and display, some are available as small as 8 point size. Since the letters are "ready made," they are easy to use and apply and no investment is required for machines and equipment.

Fig. 14.11: Transfer Lettering.

TEMPLATE LETTERING. Template lettering is produced with a stylus pen used in conjunction with a lettering template (*Fig. 14.12*) and is available in many typefaces and sizes. It is useful in preparing original art such as graphs, charts, etc.

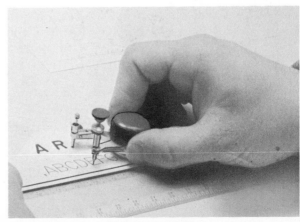

Fig. 14.12: Leroy Lettering—Template.

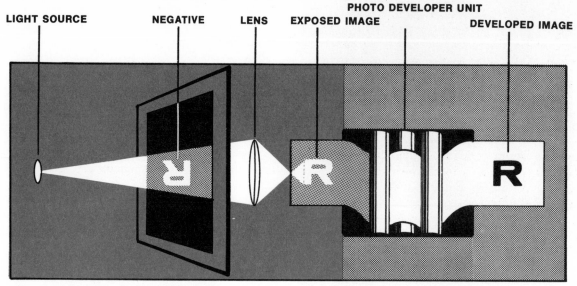

Fig. 14.13: Principle of Photo Typesetting.

Phototypesetting

We might compare traditional relief or letter-press type with phototypesetting by saying that in the latter a negative film font replaces the traditional relief metal font, liquid developer replaces the ink, and photopaper or film replaces the proofing paper. A schematic of the process is shown above (*Fig. 14.13*). The capabilities and advantages of the photo-typesetting systems are numerous. Briefly summarized, they are:

1. *Speed* of production.
2. *Direct imaging* on paper or film, positive or negative, in strip, roll or sheet form.
3. *Versatility* of letter forms, sizes, spacing and arrangement, primarily through the use of sizing and distortion lenses and because of freedom from hot type's restrictive metal relief structure.
4. *Only one set of alphanumeric characters* is required per font, as the negative image makes as many impressions as necessary through repeated exposures. Relative cost of original type is consequently low and inventory small.
5. *Uniformity and consistency* of type image and sharpness: no worn or broken type as in metal; no ink smear, spread or bleed on phototype proofs.
6. *Easy type mixing capabilities*, even on the same line, because of accessibility of negative fonts and image positioning flexibility.
7. *Clean and quiet* operation: no metal casting; no press proofing.
8. *Lightweight and compact* equipment and type: "office" style desk and cabinet equipment.
9. *Keyboarding can be done by typists* instead of skilled typesetters.
10. *Computer operation* capabilities and tie-ins.
11. In third generation systems, *fully electronic letter imaging* with cathode ray tube, eliminating need for negative fonts and providing "self font making" ability.
12. *White space is free*: there is no furniture and lock-up as in hot type.
13. *Pi (special) character availability* is simple and inexpensive.

One disadvantage should be noted: *after being set*, it is more difficult to correct or make changes in phototypesetting than in letterpress type.

Phototypesetting machines and systems range from simple, inexpensive, manually controlled units to highly complex, very expensive, extremely fast electronic systems capable of setting a whole newspaper page in minutes. Between these two extremes there are almost unlimited variations, degrees of complexity, specific applications, peripheral equipment and price ranges. Most of the developments in design, production and application have occurred in the past few years.

Fig. 14.14.

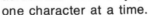

A PHOTOTYPESETTING OPERATION

The phototypesetter shown in *Fig. 14.14* is a Compugraphic, used by Denton Publications to set type for seven weekly newspapers plus some job work. This unit is capable of setting type from 5 to 24 points—text and small headlines—on lines up to 45 picas wide; the type is produced as positive proofs on photopaper 3 inches to 8 inches wide. It will set 8-point type, 11 picas wide, with leading from 1 to 31 points (in ½-point increments), at the rate of 25 lines per minute. Each negative font strip has two typefaces of 90 characters each. Type sizes and type fonts can be changed in seconds. When it was purchased, this unit cost under $8,000.

The copy to be set is first keyboarded (*Fig. 14.15*) on a tape perforating machine that "translates" characters and format information into punched codes on a tape (*Fig. 14.16*). (The perforator is not part of the typesetter, but a separate unit.) The tape is then inserted in

Fig. 14.17.

Fig. 14.15.

Fig. 14.16.

front of the electric eye of the typesetter. The operator pushes a "prime" button, then a "start" button (*Fig. 14.17*). As the tape feeds across the electric eye, the type is rapidly exposed to photopaper, one character at a time.

Fig. 14.18.

Fig. 14.19.

The machine stops automatically at the end of the coded tape, and the operator removes the cassette (*Fig. 14.18*) which contains the exposed but not yet developed type proof. This is transferred to an automatic photoprocessor, from which the proof emerges minutes later in a damp-dry condition (*Fig. 14.19*), ready for paste-up with other copy.

Photos by S. R. Maurello, Courtesy of Denton Publications

Fig. 14.21 A: Working from simply coded original...

Fig. 14.22: Recorded tape is placed in MT Reader Unit.

Fig. 14.23: Operator simply enters composing instructions at Composing Control Panel.

Fig. 14.21B: Copy is typed on IBM "Selectric" Typewriter producing proofreading copy. At the same time copy is recorded on magnetic tape.

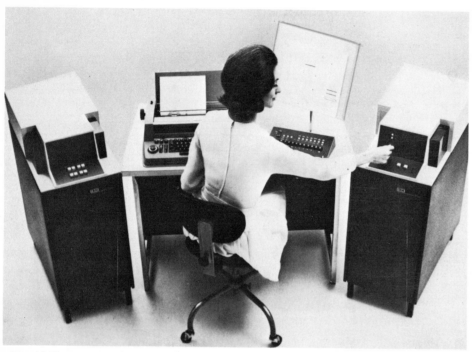

Fig. 14.20

Fig. 14.24: Operator sets up MT "Selectric" Composer . . . then monitors typesetting.

Fig. 14.25: Camera-ready copy is composed automatically.

"Strike-on" Type

Lettering produced by an ordinary typewriter differs from printer's type in that the characters of the typewriter each take up the same amount of space, whereas the space taken up by printer's type varies according to the individual letter and is known as proportional lettering. This difference partially accounts for the more uniform spacing and appearance of printer's type and its ability to be *justified*—spaced out to fill a line of specific length. Typewriterlike machines with proportional width letters and the ability to justify are known as "strike-on" or "direct image" type machines. They use a carbon-coated plastic ribbon for sharp, solid letter imaging. The Varityper and the IBM Selectric Composer are examples of such machines. Like printer's type, the typeface and

size—within a 6-point to 14-point size range—can be changed on these machines. With the aid of peripheral equipment, the IBM Selectric Composer also has magnetic tape storage and computer control capabilities. "Strike-on" machines can set text and small captions in varied formats and are very useful in making up business forms and tabulated information. They are not printing machines, but produce reproduction type for printing and also set type directly on paper printing plates for offset printing. They are used in offices, in company-owned copy preparation or printing departments and in small commercial printing firms. A very brief summary of the operation of the IBM Selectric Composer is given in *Figs. 14.20-14.25*.

82

Transfer Lettering

Type and "hand lettered" characters are available in printed form on sheets of paper or acetate with a precoated adhesive backing (*Figs. 14.26-14.27*). When lightly rubbed with a blunt pencil point or stylus, the letters can be transferred individually (see next page) in proper sequence and position, to form words on the desired surface. They are known, naturally, as "transfer letters," but are manufactured under many trade names such as Pres-type, Deca-dry, Artype, Para-type, etc. Fabricationwise, they differ in the support material on which they are printed and in the adhesive with which they are coated to make transfer possible. The support material can be translucent paper, transparent paper, frosted acetate or clear acetate and can be either thin or fairly thick. The adhesive is usually wax or rubber cement. The sheet is coated in such a manner that only the letters transfer, not the ground adhesive surrounding them. The kind that has a clear acetate support and a rubber cement adhesive is excellent to work with.

Alphabets are available in all typefaces and sizes from 8 point to 288 point; in black and white; with transparent and opaque colored letters; and with matte and shiny surfaces. Sample type catalogues are supplied by the dealers for reference and selection. Most sheets are either approximately 8″ x 13″ or 13″ x 16″ in size, identified as single- and double-size sheets respectively and priced accordingly. They have either a protective backing sheet or an envelope to prevent damage to the letters and drying out of the adhesive, which is a problem where long storage or dry atmosphere prevails.

Transfer letters are excellent for use on presentations, displays, overhead transparencies, art for reproduction and publication, charts, posters, packaging designs, TV art, labels, signs, etc. They are particularly useful for applying to colored grounds and to transparent overlays because only the *letter* transfers, allowing the ground on which it is applied to remain completely visible except where the letter covers it, just as in printing and hand lettering.

Transfer letters can be applied directly to paper offset plates (direct masters) for printing. Material prepared with transfer letters can also be used for electronic stencil-cutting machines for mimeograph duplication, as well as for office copiers, thermal and dry photo and diazo machines, used for making overhead transparencies or duplicate copies. Some brands do not withstand infra-red heat treatment; those which do are identified as heat resistant, but I have found this undependable.

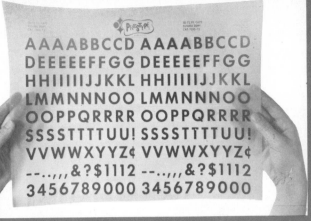

Fig. 14.26: A Sheet of Transfer Letters.

Fig. 14.27: Various Transfer Letters.

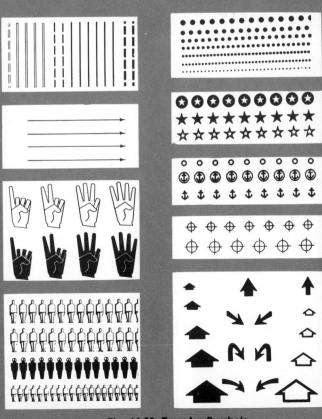

Fig. 14.28: Transfer Symbols.

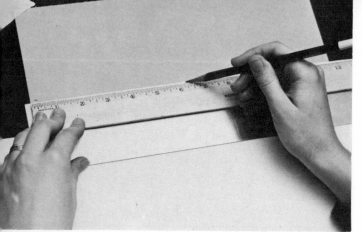

Fig. 14.29.

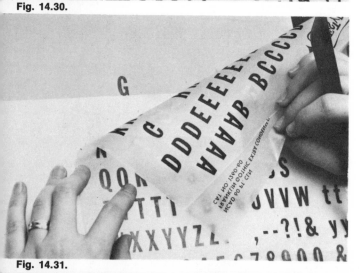

Fig. 14.30.

Fig. 14.31.

Fig. 14.32.

PROCEDURE

The object of this exercise is to center the title "BIOLOGY 101" on a gray, 9″ x 12″ TV card using a 60-point Futura Demi-bold face. The word "BIOLOGY" will be in black and the letters "101" in white, as on the completed card in *Fig. 14.33*.

The straight edge of a sheet of white paper is used as the base line for our lettering, as this can be seen more clearly through the translucent transfer sheet. Position it with a T-square and secure it with masking tape. On this white edge mark off the center at 6 inches (*Fig. 14.29*).

Remove the backing paper from the transfer lettering sheet, if it has one.

To center the title, start with the middle letter and proceed from it to the right (*Fig. 14.30*). Optically, the middle falls between O and G so place the G just to the right of the center mark, with the base of the letter just a hairline above the edge of the white guide sheet. The G is transferred by rubbing with the blunt end of a stylus. Lift the lettering sheet (*Fig. 14.31*) and shift the lettering sheet so the Y is properly positioned to the right of the G. Then transfer the Y in the same manner as the G.

Since the succeeding numbers are to be white we could either proceed with the letters to the *left* of G, to avoid changing lettering sheets, or change now to the sheet with white letters, which we shall do. Place the number 1 in position and transfer it (*Fig. 14.32*). Continue to the right, completing the white numerals.

Returning to the black lettering sheet, proceed leftward from the O to complete the word "BIOLOGY" (*Fig. 14.33*). Place tracing paper over the lettering and rub it firmly with the round end of the stylus or your thumbnail to secure it.

BIOLOGY 101

Fig. 14.33.

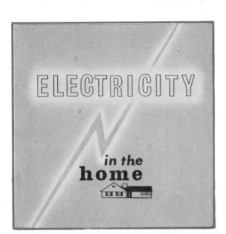

Fig. 14.34: An Overhead Transparency.

Fig. 14.35: A Printed Report Cover.

Some examples of the use of transfer letters for actual production are shown on this page. The broad range and varied applications of transfer lettering are only partially represented by these few examples.

Fig. 14.36: A Television Visual.

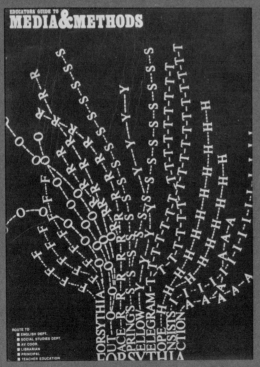

Fig. 14.39: Publication.

Fig. 14.37: A Label.

Fig. 14.38: Package.

Fig. 14.40: Courtesy of Eastman Kodak Co.

Typography

The dictionary defines typography as "1. The arrangement of composed type, or the appearance of printed matter. 2. The act and art of composing and printing from type." We shall define typography as the selection of specific typefaces or letter forms, in appropriate sizes, to be used in the planned arrangement and spacing of characters, words and lines within a given area. Good typography is that which is easily read, is inviting to read and fits the mood, style and context of the message to be conveyed in the selected medium. Granted that some of these qualities are the result of habit or current style, the definition and criteria still apply. It is often said (by persons other than typographic designers) that the reader is unconcerned about the typeface, format or paper used in printed materials; but this does not mean that these factors have neither importance nor effect. Most reading is actually done as an obligation—for study, information or business reasons—rather than as recreation or entertainment, and therefore a psychological barrier already exists between the reader and the page or other medium even before starting. Any graphic or typographic means that will "ease the pain" or make the reading more inviting and easier to comprehend and absorb is a commendable and justifiable effort, especially in this age of "picture" readers. Have you not often faced a page of solid, small type with the attitude "Must I struggle through all this?"; and have you not, on the other hand, seen a page that, by its very appearance, invited reading? However, good typography cannot overcome an author's poor thought organization or poor verbal expression; the text may be more legible and more appealing to look at, perhaps, but mentally just as indigestible.

Type in Use

In the accompanying reproduction of a page from a magazine (*Fig. 14.39*) you will note various features concerning the type:

The letters vary in *style* or structure: Some letters are made up of thin and thick strokes (1); others have strokes of uniform thickness throughout (2).

The letters vary in *size*: Some are large, others are of medium size, and some are small.

The letters vary in *weight*: Some are bold or heavy (2) compared to the overall size of the letter; others are light and thin of stroke (1).

The letters vary in *proportion*: Some are tall and narrow (2); others are as wide as they are tall (3).

The letters vary in the *direction* of the vertical strokes: Some are upright (2); others are slanted forward (1).

The letters vary in *treatment*: Most are solid black (1); others are gray in tone (5); and others are in outline (4).

The letters vary in *form*: They may be either capital letters or lower case. Some words consist of all capital letters; others of all small letters (lower case); and some have the first letter capitalized but the rest small. Letters vary in the use of *serifs* (small ornamental lines that flourish off the main strokes of letters): Some have serifs (1) and some do not (4).

In identifying and selecting letters or type for use, we consider and utilize all these features. By means of such typographic aspects, we provide legibility, emphasis, interest, variety and mood, and also allow for the limitations or mechanics of the space in which the type is used, the distance from which it is to be viewed and the particular function it is to perform. These factors encompass the design aspects of type application; they determine the choices and decisions the designer or user makes, regardless of the method of letter or type production. When working in the same medium, with fairly uniform and consistent applications and objectives, these decisions can be formalized and restricted; but when working in different media, with different objectives and applications, one's resources are taxed, especially if creativity and unity are required.

THE ART DIRECTORS SHOW · 2

The Sensitive Area: Judging

If a crucial moment of truth exists in mounting and staging an art directors show, it occurs in the two or three days devoted to judging. Hanging in balance are—recognition for the submitting artist—the success of the show itself—the burden of decision on the men who judge 👁 *It is a cool, appraising eye. An engraver's proof. A decision. A show steward bending to place the proof in an "accepted" bin. Or in the one labelled "rejected." Much discussion. Balloting. A few medals* 👁👁

CA, February '60

Fig. 14.39.

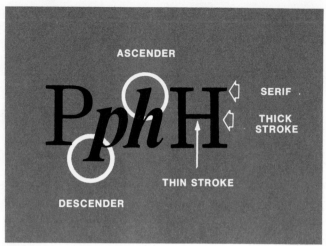

ASCENDER

SERIF

THICK STROKE

THIN STROKE

DESCENDER

Fig. 14.40.

Typefaces

The various configurations of the characters and numerals of the alphabet are basically the same for hot and cold type methods as well as for hand lettering and prefabricated lettering. In terms of broad configurations, we can classify type style or design as falling into four major categories; a catch-all fifth category covers the deviations. You will find in books on lettering or typography that the typeface categories and nomenclature are not consistently agreed upon. I have classified according to the broad structural forms that characterize or identify the type, regardless of minor developmental or historic variations. This is more consistent and less confusing than most identifying systems.

ROMAN. The first letter form shown in the accompanying chart (*Fig. 14.41*) is the Roman form, consisting of letters made of thick and thin strokes and ending in serifs. When first used as type, the alphabet consisted of capital letters only. *Lower case* Roman letters were not used in typesetting until they were introduced by Aldus Manutius, a Venetian who died in the early part of the sixteenth century. At present the Roman faces are used more than any other in printing, particulary in text applications. Within the Roman face there are many typeface variations: differences between the weight of the thick and thin strokes; changes in the curvature and thickness of the serifs; longer and shorter ascenders and descenders as compared with the body of the letter, etc. The major subdivisions are identified as Old Style (seventeenth century), Traditional (eighteenth century) and Modern.

SANS-SERIF AND SQUARE SERIF. A second letter form category consists of those letters of uniform width stroke. Those without serifs are known as sans-serif faces; those with serifs are known as square-serif faces, because the serifs are the same weight as the strokes. Usually square-serif and sans-serif types are classified in two separate typeface categories. Sans-serif faces are sometimes known as "Gothic," but historically this is a misnomer since the sans-serif letters were popularized by the German Bauhaus designers in the 1920's. At first sans-serif type was used primarily in poster design and for captions, but now it is being used more and more for text, especially where a contemporary feeling or style is desired.

SCRIPT AND CURSIVE. The third category, script and cursive, is based on handwriting and calligraphy. Script letters differ from cursive in that script letters are connected to each other when used in word form. These faces are used for announcements, invitations, poetry and advertisements of a personal, gracious or feminine nature.

TEXT OR GOTHIC. The fourth category covers "text letter"—also known as "black letter" and "Gothic"—which was used for Gutenberg's first movable type printing and was the form used by scribes and monks for the hand-lettered books that preceded printing. It is rarely used today except for religious matter and such formal printed matter as diplomas, certificates and testimonial presentations.

NOVELTY. This category covers deviations and embellishments that do not strictly fit into any of the four standard categories.

CATEGORY	STRUCTURE	EXAMPLES
Roman	Letters are made up of thick and thin strokes. AB ab	abcdefghijklmnopqrst uvwxy ABCDEFGH IJKLMNOPQRSTU
Sans-serif ······· Square serif	Letters are uniform in thickness throughout, including serifs, if any. Ab Ab	abcdefghijklm nopqr ABCDE FGHIJKLMNO
Script ······· *Cursive*	Letters are joined, as in handwriting. Handwriting character, but not joined. Ab Ab	abcdefghijklmnopqrstuvw xyz ABCDEFGH IJKLMNO 123456
Text	Manuscript letters with strong bold downstrokes and thin cross-strokes. AB ab	abcdefghijklmnopqrstuv wxyz ABCDEFGHI JKLMNOPQRST
NOVELTY	Variations or embellishments of standard letter forms; decorative or novelty. AB AB	abcdefghijklmnopqrstu vwxyz ABCDEFGHIJK QRSTUVWXYZ& 1234

Fig. 14.41: Typefaces.

WEIGHT	PROPORTION	DIRECTION

ABC
LIGHT

ABCD
MEDIUM

ABC
BOLD

Fig. 14.42A: The same typeface is often made in different weights, designated as Light, Medium, Bold and Extra Bold, so that the same design may be used for materials of varied character or connotation, or with different emphasis.

ABCDE abcde
CONDENSED

ABCDE
NORMAL

ABCDE
EXTENDED

Fig. 14.42B: To accommodate horizontal space limitations or needs, the same typefaces are made in condensed, normal and extended versions, retaining the same point height.

ABCD
abcdef
UPRIGHT

ABCD
abcde
ITALIC

Fig. 14.42C: Many typefaces are made in an Italic form (forward slanting) as well as the standard Upright (known also as Roman) form. Italics may be used for emphasis, for differentiation of context or for variety of design and "color."

Fig. 14.43: A Type Family—Variations of the Same Typeface.

FOLIO LIGHT	abcdefghij klmnopqrstuvwxyz ABCDEFGHIJKL MNOPQRRSTUVWXYZ $¢1234567890&.,:;'-)!?"" <small>Ligatures ff, fi, fl available in sizes from 6 to 14 point</small>	**FOLIO LIGHT CONDENSED**	abcdefghij klmnopqrstuvwxyz ABCDEFGHIJKL MNOPQRRSTUVWXYZ $¢1234567890 &.,:;'-)!?""	
FOLIO LIGHT ITALIC	*abcdefghij klmnopqrstuvwxyz ABCDEFGHIJKL MNOPQRSTUVWXYZ $¢1234567890&.,:;'-)!?""* <small>Ligatures ff, fi, fl available in sizes from 6 to 14 point</small>	**FOLIO MEDIUM CONDENSED**	abcdefghij klmnopqrstuvwxyz ABCDEFGHIJKL MNOPQRRSTUVWXYZ $¢1234567890 &.,:;'-)!?""	
FOLIO MEDIUM	abcdefghij klmnopqrstuvwxyz ABCDEFGHIJKL MNOPQRRSTUVWXYZ $¢1234567890&.,:;'-)!?"" <small>Ligatures ff, fi, fl available in sizes from 6 to 14 point</small>	**FOLIO BOLD CONDENSED**	abcdefghij klmnopqrstuvwxyz ABCDEFGHIJKL MNOPQRRSTUVWXYZ $¢1234567890 &.,:;'-)!?""	
FOLIO BOLD	**abcdefghij klmnopqrstuvwxyz ABCDEFGHIJKL MNOPQRRSTUVWXYZ $¢1234567890&.,:;'-)!?""**	**FOLIO MEDIUM EXTENDED**	abcdefghij klmnopqrstuvwxyz ABCDEFGHIJKL MNOPQRRSTUVWXYZ $¢1234567890 &.,:;'-)!?""	
FOLIO EXTRABOLD	**abcdefghij klmnopqrstuvwxyz ABCDEFGHIJKL MNOPQRRSTUVWXYZ $¢1234567890 &.,:;'-)!?""**	**FOLIO MEDIUM EXTENDED ITALIC**	*abcdefghij klmnopqrstuvwxyz ABCDEFGHIJKL MNOPQRRSTUVWXYZ $¢1234567890&.,:;'-)!?""*	

2 POINTS

Fig. 14.45.

Type Measurement

Type is measured in *point* sizes, using the vertical dimension. A point is approximately 1/72nd of an inch; thus, 72-point type would be about an inch high. However, since the measurement is based on relief metal type and relates to the height of the metal block that carries the relief letter, the actual *image* of a 72-point-type letter will not be 1 inch high. A comparison of the metal type pieces and their inked images in *Figs. 14.44-14.45* shows the reason for the apparent disparity. Note also that the *capital* letter does not take up the full height of the metal block. The full height of the type measurement is from the top of an ascender letter, such as "b," to the bottom of a descender letter, such as "g." No modern letter has both an ascender and descender.

This creates another seeming discrepancy in type size appearance, because some typefaces are designed with long ascenders and descenders, while others have short ones, with the body size of the letter varying to make up the difference. *Fig. 14.45*, for example, illustrates the optical size discrepancy in such a situation; both sets of letters are in 72-point type, but the lower case letters on the right seem taller. In text setting this would be even more apparent. A typeface design is available in different point sizes. The range of sizes is known as a type series (*Fig. 14.46*).

Although the physical form of the type and the process of letter imaging differ between relief metal type and phototypography, they use the same method of type measurement and the same basic typeface designs.

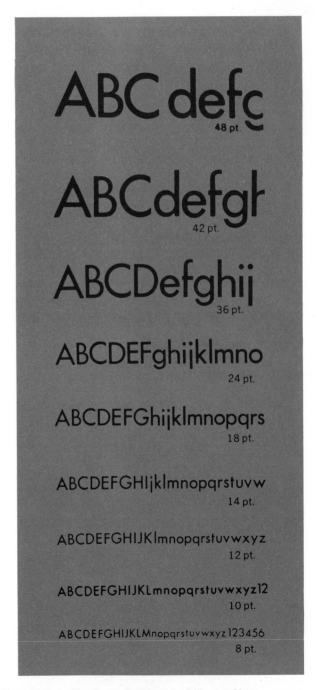

Fig. 14.46: A Type Series—The Same Typeface in Different Sizes.

Copy Fitting

Text and captions which are to be set in type for printing or duplication generally originate in the form of typewritten copy, although they may also exist in handwritten or even in some previously printed form. Since this material, when typeset, will almost invariably be of different character size, line length and between-line spacing, it will require a different size and shape area than the original copy (*Figs. 14.48, 14.52-14.53*). The procedure for determining *how much space will be required* by the copy when set in type or *how to set* the copy so it will fit into a *designated space* is known as "copy fitting."

For casting purposes we may classify type in two categories: display type and body type. The former consists of headings and subheadings, usually large type of short wordage, and the latter usually consists of text grouped as a unit or divided into units of different sizes.

Most display type (*Fig. 14.47*) can be measured easily and quickly by counting off the individual characters in a line (including the spaces between words), then selecting, from a type book, a particular typeface and size and finally measuring the same number of characters in that face and size. This will give the length of the heading when set in type. If the line is slightly long or short, it can often be condensed or enlarged by deleting or adding spaces.

Copy fitting is based on character count, which includes punctuation marks and spaces (*Fig. 14.50*). Since each character of a *typewriter* alphabet takes up the *same amount* of horizontal space, there will be the same number of characters in each line of the same length. If we multiply the number of characters on each line by the number of lines, we arrive at the total number of characters on a typewritten page or within a selected area of a page. Although *type characters for printing vary in width* according to the particular character (an m is wider than an i), in a group of lines of the same length they average the same count for the same typeface and type size. It can thus be determined either *how many characters* will fit into any given length line or what line length will be required for any given number of characters. Character count tables for specific typefaces and sizes provide the basis for computation (*Fig. 14.51*). Many typographers and printers supply to their clients catalogues with

30 Point Stymie Bold Italic

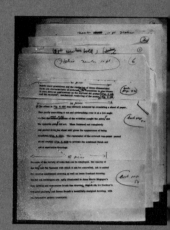

FULL SIZE

Fig. 14.47: Measuring Display Type.

Fig. 14.48: Printed Page and Manuscript.

Fig. 14.49.

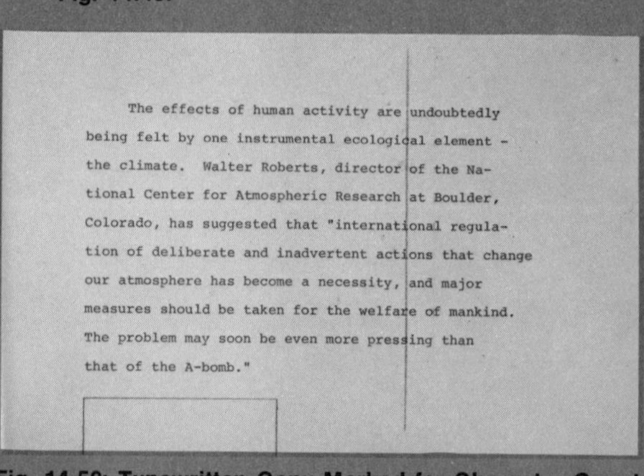

Fig. 14.50: Typewritten Copy Marked for Character Count.

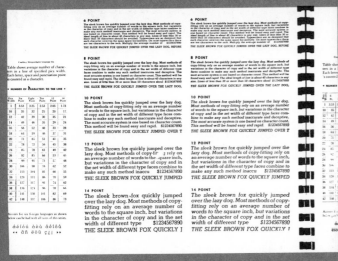

Fig. 14.51: Page from a Type Catalogue. A Type Speciman Sheet.

CHARACTER COUNT

Table shows average number of characters in a line of specified pica width. Each letter, space and punctuation point is counted as a character.

Pica Width	6 Pt.	7 Pt.	8 Pt.	9 Pt.	10 Pt.	11 Pt.	12 Pt.	14 Pt.
1	3.5	3.2	3.0	2.8	2.6	2.3	2.0	1.8
10	35	32	30	28	26	23	20	18
12	42	38	36	33	31	27	24	21
14	49	44	42	38	36	31	28	24
16	56	50	48	43	41	35	32	27
18	64	56	54	48	46	39	36	30
20	71	62	60	53	51	43	40	33
22	77	68	66	58	56	47	44	36
24	84	76	72	63	61	51	48	39
26	91	82	78	68	66	55	52	42
28	98	88	84	73	71	59	56	45
30	105	94	90	78	76	63	60	48
32	112	100	96	83	81	67	64	51
34	119	106	112	88	86	71	68	54
36	126	112	118	93	91	75	72	57

type samples and reference tables for selecting and fitting the type they service or stock. Several commercially produced manuals for this purpose are also available.

The following factors are involved in copy fitting: (1) The specific typeface to be used. (2) The point size of the type to be used. (3) The length of line to be set, or width of space to be used. (4) The amount of leading (spaces between lines), if any. (5) The amount of copy to be set.

PROCEDURE

Assume that we are required to fit the copy in *Fig. 14.52* into a space 18 picas wide, and we need to determine what depth is required. Consulting a type book, we select an 8-point Memphis Medium Italic (*Fig. 14.51*). From the table in the type book, we note that there are 54 characters to an 18-pica line for this type and size. Going back to the typewritten copy, count off 54 characters (including spaces and punctuation) in the top line, and through this point draw a vertical pencil line down the page. Count the number of full lines of copy, and add to it the number of lines made up by the characters to the right of the vertical line and the characters in the short line. The total amounts to four and a half lines.

To determine the depth of the printed text, add the point size of the type—8 points—to the amount of spacing desired between lines—in this case, 2-point leading—which gives a total of 10 points per line. Since there are five lines this makes a total of 50 points (actually 48 points since there is no leading below the fifth line). Since there are 12 points to a pica this will be a depth of 4 picas, or about five-eighths of an inch (*Fig. 14.53*).

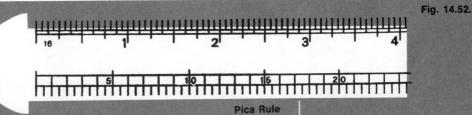

In all the years of typographic development, there has been one outstanding rule that governed the progress of the art, namely simplicity. This does not mean that everything should be plain or unattractive, unappealing or drab. It means just neat and effective.

Fig. 14.52.

Pica Rule

Fig. 14.53.

In all the years of typographic development, there has been one outstanding rule that governed the progress of the art, namely, simplicity. This does not mean everything should be plain or unattractive, unappealing or drab. It means just neat and effective.

15. Design and Layout

WITH REGARD to communication graphics, we might consider design to be the visual interpretation and form given to illustrative and/or verbal material used to convey a message (*Fig. 15.1*). The message might serve to impartially inform, as would the news content of a newspaper, magazine or television broadcast; it might serve to convince or sell, as would an advertisement, brochure or billboard; it might serve to instruct, as would a textbook or visual aid; it might serve to identify, as would a sign, a letterhead, etc. The important aspects for the designer to consider are:

1. *What is the message* to be conveyed?
2. *To whom* is it directed?
3. *By what means* will it be conveyed; that is, what medium and what particular form within that medium (see page 110)?

Other aspects related to these are: to how many persons must this message by conveyed; over how long a period will this message be pertinent; how much can be spent for the purpose; is visual motion necessary; is color necessary, etc. Obviously, many of these factors will have been decided upon before the designer is given the assignment; nevertheless they are matters that the designer has to take into account.

The matter of visual interpretation, and form or arrangement of material, is interestingly shown in the designs illustrated here—four independently arrived at designs using fingerprint motifs for two advertising brochures and for two trade publication covers. Note how the same symbol, the fingerprint, is applied to different concepts—push-button, security, identity, etc—in these illustrations.

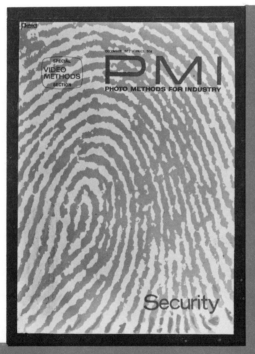

Fig. 15.1.

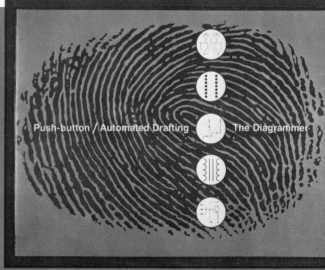

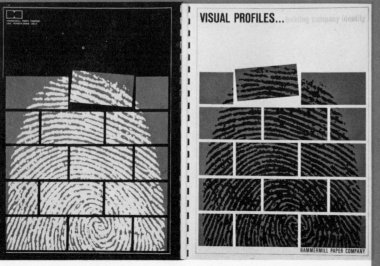

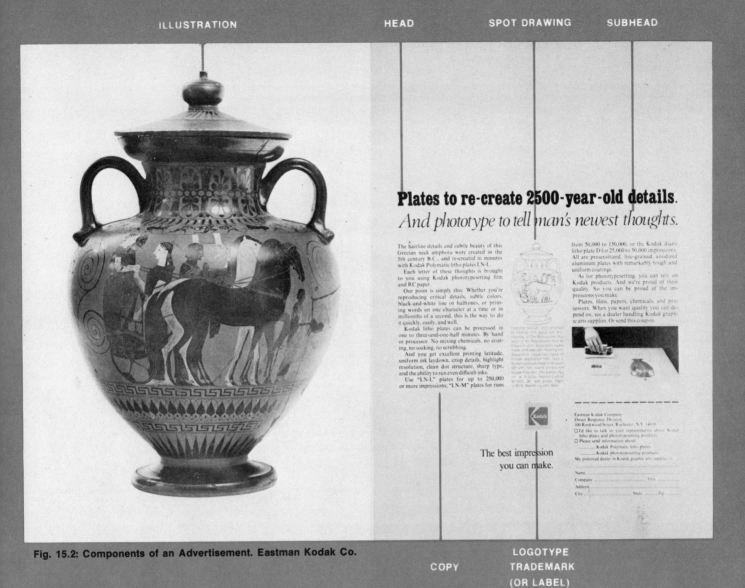

ILLUSTRATION   HEAD   SPOT DRAWING   SUBHEAD

Plates to re-create 2500-year-old details.
And phototype to tell man's newest thoughts.

The hairline details and subtle beauty of this Grecian neck amphora were created in the 5th century B.C., and re-created in minutes with Kodak Polymatic litho plates LN-L.

Each letter of these thoughts is brought to you using Kodak phototypesetting film and RC paper.

Our point is simply this: Whether you're reproducing critical details, subtle colors, black-and-white line or halftones, or printing words set one character at a time or in millionths of a second, this is the way to do it quickly, easily, and well.

Kodak litho plates can be processed in one to three-and-one-half minutes. By hand or processor. No mixing chemicals, no coating, no soaking, no scrubbing.

And you get excellent printing latitude, uniform ink laydown, crisp details, highlight resolution, clean dot structure, sharp type, and the ability to run even difficult inks.

Use "LN-L" plates for up to 250,000 or more impressions; "LN-M" plates for runs

from 50,000 to 150,000; or the Kodak diazo litho plate D for 25,000 to 50,000 impressions. All are presensitized, fine-grained, anodized aluminum plates with remarkably tough and uniform coatings.

As for phototypesetting, you can rely on Kodak products. And we're proud of their quality. So you can be proud of the impressions you make.

Plates, films, papers, chemicals, and processors. When you want quality you can depend on, see a dealer handling Kodak graphic arts supplies. Or send this coupon.

The best impression you can make.

Eastman Kodak Company
Direct Response Division
100 Rockwood Street, Rochester, N.Y. 14650
☐ I'd like to talk to your representative about Kodak litho plates and phototypesetting products
☐ Please send information about
_____ Kodak Polymatic litho plates
_____ Kodak phototypesetting products
My preferred dealer in Kodak graphic arts supplies is

Name
Company _____ Title
Address
City _____ State _____ Zip

COPY   LOGOTYPE   TRADEMARK (OR LABEL)

Fig. 15.2: Components of an Advertisement. Eastman Kodak Co.

Advertisements and Their Preparation

Since a magazine or newspaper advertisement is a rather complete entity, let us examine it in detail. The various units that make up a typical advertisement are indicated above (*Fig. 15.2*).

Not all ads have all these units, and other ads may have several more units of copy and several illustrations. Some principles must be adhered to in deciding upon the size, form and placement of these individual items. Since the primary function of an ad is to sell or promote something—merchandise, service, good will, information or a concept—the ad, first of all,

should attract *attention*. It is necessary to have all units seen, and seen in some particular order; so *movement* is another factor to consider. Some particular idea or object should dominate, therefore the ad should have *emphasis*, but in such a manner that *balance* is maintained, otherwise the reader will go no further. To do all this and keep the ad together as a whole, *unity* should be achieved. Yet, despite all these various factors, the ad should be *simple*, not complicated and confusing.

Fig. 15.3:
The Thumbnail Sketch.

Fig. 15.4: The Rough.

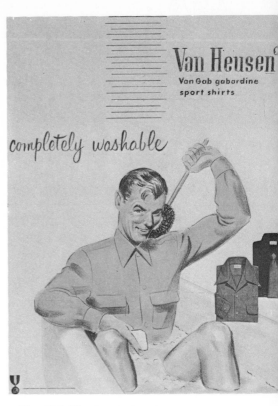

Fig. 15.5: The Comprehensive.

Steps in Preparing an Ad

The steps in preparing an advertisement vary with the kind of ad, the requirements of the client, the funds and time available for that particular project, and the type of staff available. The major stages of the work are:

THUMBNAIL SKETCHES. The thumbnail sketch (*Fig. 15.3*) is a small, quick sketch made to determine the general form the ad will take. Several of these are briefly made with pencil, crayon or pastel on layout paper, varying them as much as possible or refining some preconceived idea.

ROUGH. The rough (*Fig. 15.4*) is a more detailed sketch of the one or two best ideas selected from the thumbnails. The rough should be done the same size that the printed ad will appear. Illustrations and lettering on roughs are generally indicated in a bold, simplified technique with soft pencil, felt pen, hard pastel or colored pencil, and an occasional touch of tempera. Without being sloppy or amateurish looking, the rendering of a rough has a quick and incisive character that is easily distinguishable from the painstaking, detailed rendering of the finish. In *Fig. 15.4* the "layout technique" is identifiable as such. The

pencil can be handled as indicated on pages 16-18 and pastel as on page 44. Tempera is useful when indicating colored or reverse lettering on a pastel background. Smooth white bond paper, either opaque or semi-transparent, and tracing paper are used for layouts.

The art director or client will check the rough, and either suggest modifications, ask for other ideas, or approve.

COMPREHENSIVE. The comprehensive (*Fig. 15.5*) or "comp," a step closer to the finish than the rough, is made for the more complicated or expensive type of ad, especially if the client wants to see exactly what he's getting before he gets it. Sometimes the illustrative portion is carried so far one almost wonders why it isn't used as a finish. Often this step is omitted, and the artist or art director proceeds from rough to finished art (*Fig. 15.6*).

MECHANICAL. The mechanical (*Fig. 15.7*) is a composite of the separate finished units of which the printed ad will consist. In their original state these units may be the same size or larger (rarely smaller) than the work will appear when reproduced. Different units for

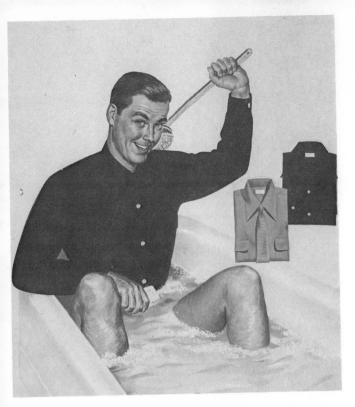

Fig. 15.6: The Finished Illustration.

Fig. 15.7: The Mechanical.

the same ad may be scaled differently. For instance, the type may be the same size as it will appear in the finish, separate hand lettering may have been done one and a half times larger, a photo may be twice up, and the original art for the illustration, three times larger. These units are photostated or photographed to the size in which they will appear in the ad and then combined with whatever originals are already in scale. This combination of pasted-up units is known as the "mechanical" (see Chapter 16); it serves both as a guide to the engraver for assembling the various units in the plates and, sometimes, as copy for his camera. The various units may be photographed separately by the copy photographer at the printing plant, each being reduced to the finish size, and all combined together on the "flats" from which the plates for printing are made. This is a very brief and oversimplified manner of describing a complicated process. It actually belongs to the domain of the production man, but the commercial artist should have some conception of the processes through which his work must be put. While I have used the term "advertisement" in describing the above procedure, very much the same course would be followed for a brochure, a book jacket, label, etc.

Fig. 15.8: The Reproduced Ad. Robert Bennett, Grey Advertising Agency,   Philip Jones Corp.

completely washable

Van Heusen

Van Gab gabardine sport shirts

Fig. 15.9: Window Display.

Although newspapers and magazines are the major vehicles for printed advertisements, direct mail brochures and point-of-purchase ads are also important methods of utilizing the print medium. On this page the previously discussed magazine ad is shown in adaptations made for direct mail and point-of-purchase use, all coordinated as part of one particular advertising campaign. These are shown in reduced size.

so washable!

our **Van Gab** gabardine sport shirts by **Van Heusen**

$0.00

Tub them, scrub them —they stay smooth and soft as new...and always comfortable from collar to cuffs. Won't shrink...keep their sparkling colors. Exclusive Van Heusen California Lo-No collar looks smart, feels great . . . with or without a tie!

Dealer's Name and Address

Fashion Academy Gold Medal 1951

Fig. 15.12: Newspaper Mat for Dealers.

Fig. 15.10: Double Reply Card.

Fig. 15.11: Single Postcard.

Fig. 15.13: A Streamer.

c'mon in . . .   the water's fine for

Van Heusen
completely washable
Van Gab gabardine sport shirts

When designing materials for print, one works within certain format restrictions or decisions. "Format" pertains to the size, style, shape and form requirements or choices involved in the particular graphic piece or publication being designed. For example, not only do newspapers and magazines vary in overall size and proportion, but the individual pages are planned on the basis of column units, which are of standard width for any specific periodical but which vary from one periodical to another. Thus, the designer of newspaper ads will have varied size areas in which to prepare his ads: anywhere from a full page to 1 column wide by 1 inch deep. The newspaper ad shown in *Fig. 15.12* was planned for a space 2 columns wide by 170 lines deep, which for the average full-size newspaper is about 3½" x 20". On the other hand, a record album container is always square, because of the shape of the enclosed record. A few of the many different printed forms that advertising, identifying, informational and packaging materials may take are shown in this page.

Fig. 15.14: Map

Fig. 15.15: Program

Fig. 15.16: Letterhead.

Fig. 15.17: Advertising Folder.

Fig. 15.18: Record Album Cover.

Fig. 15.19: Business Card

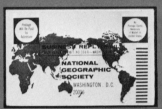

Fig. 15.20: Reply Postcard.

Fig. 15.21: Catalogue

Fig. 15.22: Flyer

Fig. 15.23: Gift-wrap

Fig. 15.24: Envelope

Fig. 15.25: Package.

16. Paste-ups and Mechanicals

WHEN PREPARING material for print as well as for some forms of nonprint reproduction, it is often necessary to assemble several units of type proofs, photographs, photostats, spot illustrations, hand lettering, logotypes, etc. (*Figs. 16.1-16.4*). Using rubber cement or an adhesive wax coating, these units are pasted in position on paper or illustration board, following a given layout; then, additional art, such as ruling pen work, minor retouching, making of corrections and drawing can be done directly on this "mechanical." The terms "paste-ups" and "mechanicals" are used to describe both the functions performed and the resulting artwork. A complete mechanical is shown on the next page. The identifying terms and leaders are not part of the mechanical, but are provided for your information.

The mechanical, with original illustrations (Fig. 16.1) was prepared for newspaper advertising, at same size as the newspaper reproduction, 13″ x 22″. It is reproduced here much smaller, and also in such manner that the paste-up edges of the various units of type and drawing appear as they do in the original mechanical; however, these cut edges and paper tonal differences are eliminated in actual reproduction, as shown in Fig. 16.2.

Fig. 16.2: The Ad as it Appeared in Newspaper Reproduction (reduced in size here). Fred Greenhill, Lord & Taylor.

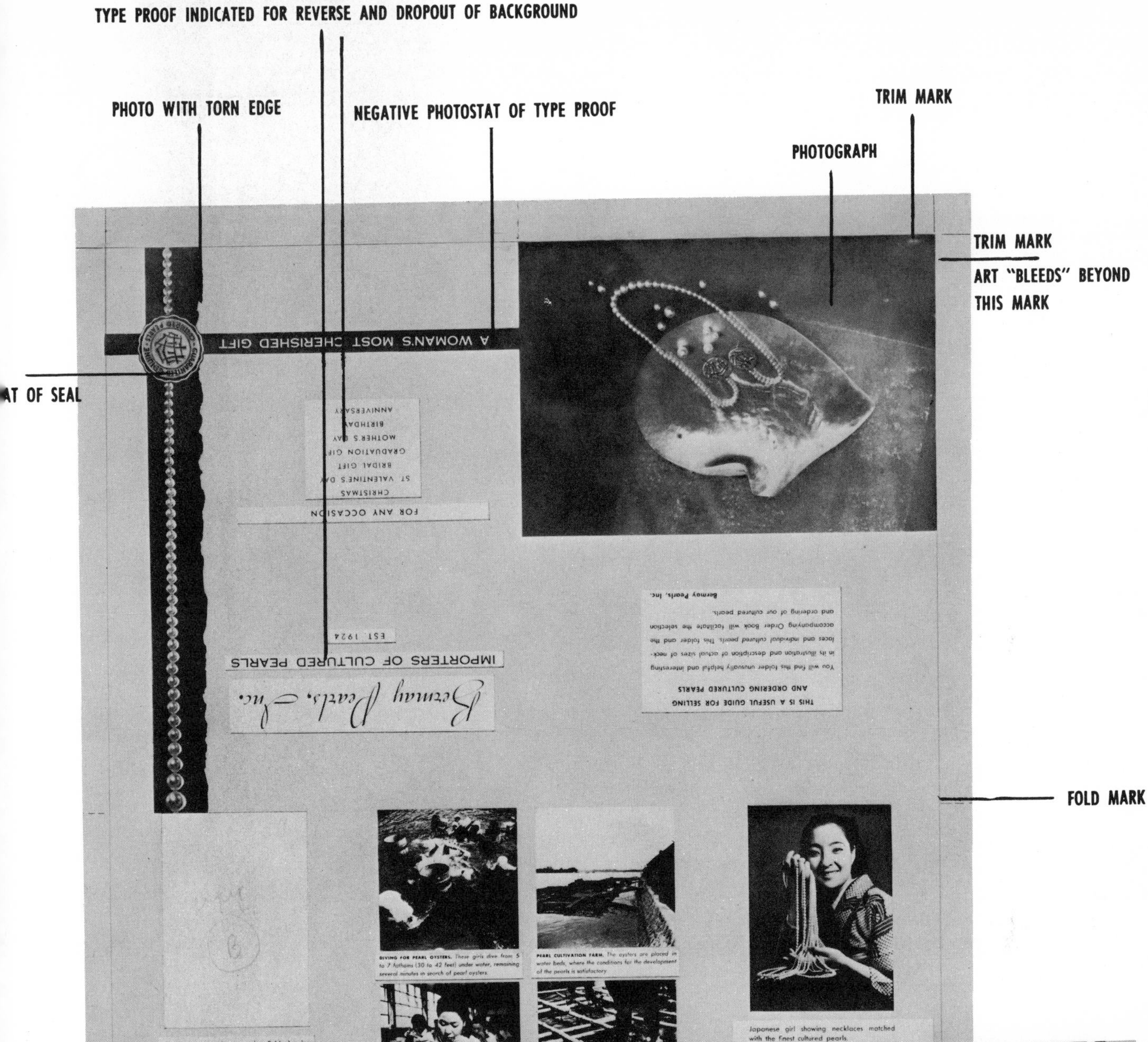

TYPE PROOF INDICATED FOR REVERSE AND DROPOUT OF BACKGROUND

PHOTO WITH TORN EDGE

NEGATIVE PHOTOSTAT OF TYPE PROOF

TRIM MARK

PHOTOGRAPH

TRIM MARK

ART "BLEEDS" BEYOND THIS MARK

AT OF SEAL

FOLD MARK

SPACE LEFT FOR OVERSIZE PHOTO WHICH WILL BE REDUCED AND STRIPPED IN POSITION

TYPE PROOF

PHOTOSTAT OF DRAWING

Fig. 16.3. A Mechanical for A Two-Color Advertising Folder.

Fig. 16.4.

101

Use of Rubber Cement

For paste-up procedures, rubber cement is used as the adhesive because it does not (or at least *should* not) leave a stain on paper, allows for repositioning of the material if necessary, is flexible when dry and can easily be removed from unwanted areas when dry. It is obtainable in art supply stores in pint or larger size cans. For use it should be transferred to a rubber cement dispenser—a glass or plastic jar with an adjustable brush in the cap (*Fig. 16.6*). The brush can be moved up or down to allow its end to remain in the rubber cement. Do not apply more rubber cement to an area than is necessary to provide a thin, even coat. If thus applied to the back of a piece of paper or a photograph that is immediately placed on the surface on which it is to be mounted (*Fig. 16.8*), the paper or photograph can be shifted, if necessary, during the minute or so before the rubber cement dries. If *both* the back of the paper and the mounting surface are coated with cement and allowed to dry before adhering, no shifting can be done, and the bond will be immediate and permanent. A rubber cement solvent or thinner is used to thin cement in a jar which has thickened upon prolonged exposure to the air. Excess rubber cement can be removed from an area after drying by rubbing it with a finger, with the tacky side of a piece of masking tape or with a lump of dried rubber cement, commonly referred to as a "pickup."

Pasting up Type

In the following exercise, we have a reproduction proof of a single line caption to paste up as a mechanical. It is also necessary to enclose the body copy with a thin pen line border (*Fig. 16.9*, arrow).

The border is inked in with a ruling pen, using a T-square and triangle. (See page 50 for ruling pen procedures.) The reproduction proof is cut out, care being taken not to cut too close to the lettering, but close enough so that the proof is not larger than the inked border (*Fig. 16.9*). This proof is wet mounted—that is, rubber cement is applied only to the back of the proof, not to the illustration board—and placed in position quickly. Note that when placing the proof in position, the sides of the proof are

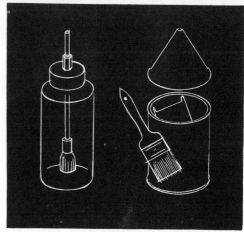

Fig. 16.5:   Various Types of Dispenser Jars.

Fig. 16.6:   Rubber Cement in Dispenser Jar.

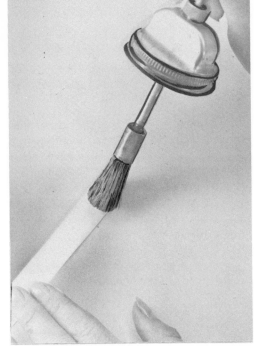

Fig. 16.7: Cutting Type Proof for Paste-up.   Fig. 16.8: Applying Rubber Cement to Back of Type Proof.

Fig. 16.9.   The Paste-up is Placed in Position.

curved upward so that only the center comes in contact with the board at first, then the two edges are allowed to drop down. The line of type is lined up using a T- square (*Fig. 16.10*). Since the rubber cement is still wet, the proof can be maneuvered into exact position if not already there. After being placed in position, the proof is covered with a sheet of tracing paper for protection and pressed firmly to the illustration board.

Fig. 16.10.

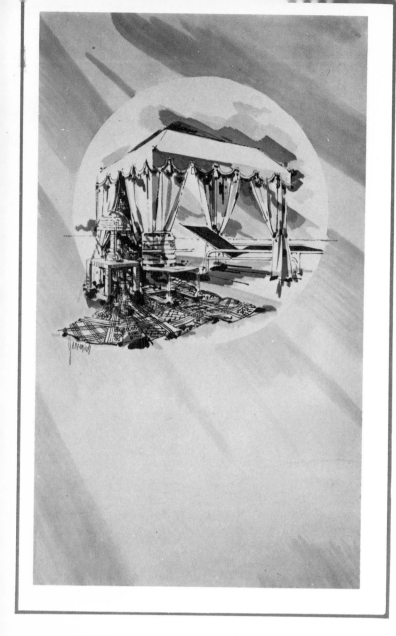

Fig. 16.11A: The Original Illustration, Continuous Tone Art, Done in Opaque Watercolor, Same Size as Newspaper Page.

Fig. 16.11B: An Acetate Overlay with Type Proof Paste-up (Line Art) Placed over Drawing, in Register. (A Sheet of Paper Has Been Placed between the Drawing and the Overlay for Clarification).

USE OF THE OVERLAY

Often material prepared for reproduction consists of artwork, photographs or type mounted on illustration board, with one or more overlays of type or additional art on tracing paper, acetate or lightweight bond paper. The overlay is prepared in register (see registration marks, *Fig.16.11A*) with the base material. The base art and overlay art are combined in the photographic or printing stages. This procedure is used to facilitate the combination of continuous tone art with line art or copy, as well as for color separation and special effects. In the example shown here we have continuous tone art (the illustration, *Fig. 16.11A)* and line art (the type, *Fig. 16.11B)* printed in such manner that the art background shows behind the block of type, *Fig. 16.11D.*

Fig. 16.11C: The Drawing with Overlay as Submitted to Printer.

Fig. 16.11 D: The Finished Reproduction.

Carlo Ammiratti, Advertising Manager, Lord & Taylor.
George Kuharski, Art Director, Lord & Taylor.
Drawing by Jeremiah Goodman

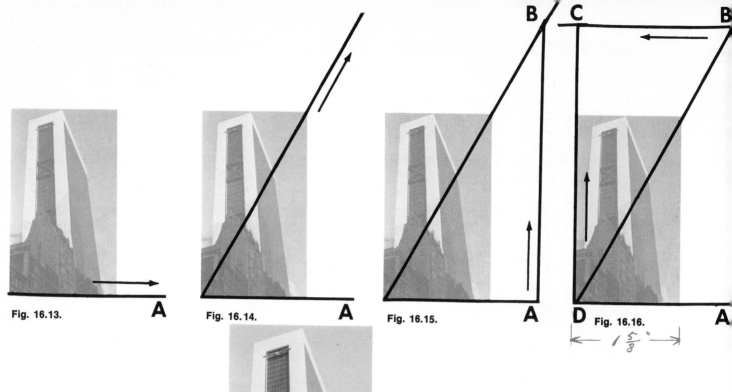

Fig. 16.13.

Fig. 16.14.

Fig. 16.15.

Fig. 16.16.

$1 \frac{5}{8}"$

Fig. 16.12.

Fig. 16.17.

Scaling

Often when preparing artwork, layouts, photographs or illustrations, it is necessary to work in a size different from the size in which the work will appear in reproduction; or, conversely, it might be necessary to determine what size to prepare the art so it will fit a page or layout when enlarged or reduced. The procedure for determing these measurements is known as *scaling*.

In *Fig. 16.12* we have a photograph that is actually *1 inch wide* by 1¾ inches high. In reproduction it will be used *1⅝ inches wide*. We must determine how much vertical space the photograph will take up at this enlarged width. This can be determined mathematically or by using a scaling device, but since the actual area involved often has to be shown, the scaling is done by placing a piece of tracing paper over the photo, adhering it at the top with masking tape or rubber cement, then determining the new size on this, using a T-square, triangle and

grease pencil or soft lead pencil, marking lightly so as not to indent the photograph if it is to be used for the actual reproduction.

PROCEDURE

Shown at actual size is the photograph that has to be scaled for enlargement (*Fig. 16.12*). A sheet of tracing paper larger than the photo is placed over the photo and held in position with masking tape (*Fig. 16.13*). Along the bottom of the photo a line is extended 1⅝ inches from the lefthand corner to point A, the width to which the photo is to be enlarged. A diagonal is drawn from the lower lefthand corner through the upper right corner (*Fig. 16.14*). From point A a vertical line is erected till it intersects the diagonal, which point is marked B (*Fig. 16.15*). From B a horizontal line is extended beyond the left border of the photo (*Fig. 16.16*). From the lower lefthand corner of the photo, point D, a vertical line is erected till it intersects line CB. Measure line AB, which will be the depth of the photo when its width is enlarged as required. Note that the *new* width desired is indicated along the *current* width as a guide to the photographer, platemaker or printer.

If we were starting with a *large size* image and had to determine a reduced size we would reverse the procedure, starting with *Fig. 16.16*, and marking off the smaller width and erecting a vertical to the diagonal inside the rectangle.

If we were given the vertical dimension (known, in production terms, as *depth*) and had to determine the new width, we would start with the vertical line (line CD, *Fig. 16.16*), then draw the diagonal, extend a horizontal from point C to the diagonal. Measure the new width, CB.

olor Separation

considerable amount of print material con-
sts of two or more line (flat) colors, or one
lftone color plus flat color(s). It is more
onomical and expeditious for the original art
be prepared as "color separations." Just as
ch color is printed from a separate plate so is
e artwork prepared on correspondingly
parate sheets of paper or overlays. The
twork for the color separations is drawn in
ack ink, regardless of the final printed colors.
ter the art is photocopied and the plates
ade, each plate is inked in the color indicated
the artist's sketch or swatches on the
erlays and is printed in sequence, in register
th the previous color. Proper preparation and
gistration of the separation artwork is
cessary to assure this.

Fig. 16.18: Color Sketch.

Fig. 16.22: Two-Color Print.

ig. 16.19: Separation Drawing
or Blue Printing Plate.

Fig. 16.20: Tracing Vellum Placed Over Previous
Drawing and Black Plate Drawing Done in Exact
Register on This Overlay.

Fig. 16.21: Black Plate Drawing Overlay

ROCEDURE

color sketch of the design is made (*Fig.
6.18*), and in this particular example at the
ame size as is to be printed.

On white drawing paper or board, a drawing
or the blue areas is made in black ink (*Fig.
6.19*), *twice the size* that the drawing will be
rinted. Trim marks are accurately drawn in
ach corner of the artwork, and any color which
 to bleed is drawn at least one-eighth inch
eyond the trim.

A sheet of vellum is placed over the previous
rawing, which here appears gray as a conse-
uence (*Fig. 16.20*). The trim marks are
recisely traced in position on this overlay, and
hatever artwork is to be printed black is now

drawn in exact register with the drawing
beneath. *Fig. 16.21* shows this color separation
overlay as it actually appears.

The artwork shown in *Fig. 16.19* is now
photo copied same size in which it will be used
on the printing plate; the plate is made and
printed in blue ink. The same will be done with
the overlay drawing, and printed black over the
previous color (*Fig. 16.22*). The type, incidently,
was stripped in on the negative for the black
plate, since the type proofs were made the
same size as the final printed piece, but the
artwork was made twice the size for convenience.

17. Communications Media

IN TERMS OF general areas of use, artwork, both illustrative and verbal, falls into either of two categories: art for *direct use*, and art prepared for *reproduction*—that is, for conversion to another medium or communicative form, either through duplication, transmission or projection.

Uses of Artwork

DIRECT USE.   Artwork is used directly when it is displayed, referred to or used in its original form. The use may be transitory, such as the rendering for a newly designed product, or semi-permanent, such as artwork on an exhibition panel (*Fig. 17.1*).

REPRODUCTION USE.   Most commercial art is intended for conversion into some other image form or visual medium. This might be done for the purpose of making multiple copies, for more convenient and effective viewing, for transmission to other locations and outlets, for storage and retrieval when needed, etc. The "vehicle" used to carry the image and/or message is known as the *medium*; we speak of the "television medium," the "publications media" and many others, including nonvisual media such as radio. There are two kinds of reproduction communications media: print and nonprint.

Print vs. Nonprint Media

PRINT MEDIA refers to those communications media requiring reproduction processes in which the graphic image, verbal or illustrative, is converted to a physical form known as a printing plate, whereby the image can be inked and then transferred to paper or other material by means of a printing press (*Fig. 17.2*). This is an over-simplification, but serves our purpose for the moment.

Nonprint media refers to those communications media using reproduction processes *in which no ink image transfer occurs*, but in which the image is duplicated, transmitted or generated by photographic, thermal, chemical or electronic means. Some examples of nonprint media are: television, color slide projections (*Fig. 17.3*), office copy machine and microfilm.

artwork prepared for

DIRECT USE

print REPRODUCTION

non-print REPRODUCTION

process

media

display

direct application

Fig. 17.1.

publication

printing plate and press

Fig. 17.2.

slide viewer

camera and slide film

Fig. 17.3.

COMMUNICATIONS MEDIA

PRINT MEDIA   DIRECT IMAGE   NON PRINT MEDIA

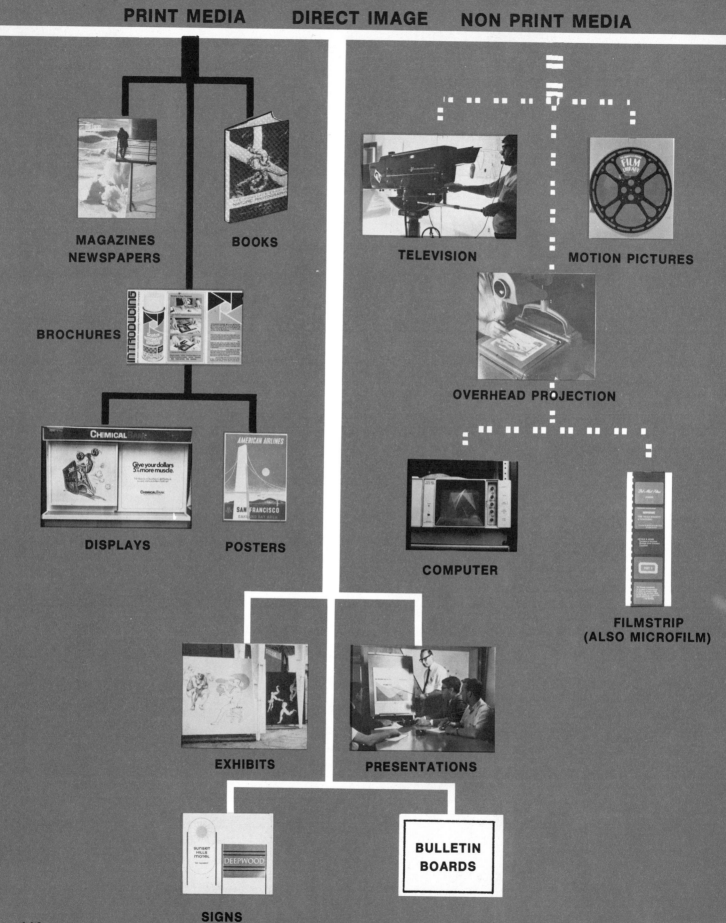

MAGAZINES
NEWSPAPERS

BOOKS

TELEVISION

MOTION PICTURES

BROCHURES

OVERHEAD PROJECTION

DISPLAYS

POSTERS

COMPUTER

FILMSTRIP
(ALSO MICROFILM)

EXHIBITS

PRESENTATIONS

SIGNS

BULLETIN
BOARDS

Graphic Communication

Fig. 17.5: Courtesy of Museum of Natural History, New York

For many centuries man had only simple means of communicating with others: hand sign language, vocal sounds, pictographs laboriously inscribed in stone—symbols which eventually developed into our written alphabets (*Fig. 17.5*). Basically, we still use the same means of communication, but through drawing and photography we have developed an imagery that has become far more representative of actual persons, scenes, objects and activities. Our images *move* and *speak*, emitting natural sounds. The ancient cuneiform tablet, time-consuming to produce, heavy, cumbersome and strictly a one-of-a-kind product, has been replaced by the newspaper, duplicated by the hundreds of thousands for a day's use; it, in turn, has been replaced by electronic images and sounds sent through the atmosphere, replicated throughout the world almost instantaneously, and by many other methods and forms of communication which we take for granted—and often consider quite inadequate (*Fig. 17.6*). We have only begun to see what the computer will put at our service (see chapter 13), with its tremendous storage capability, speed of retrieval and many output forms, including images on cathode ray tubes, drawn images and images on film. The graphic artist must certainly extend his vision and abilities beyond the drawing board, and beyond the printed page. Thorough discussion of each of these areas of communication would require a complete book; unfortunately, in this book we can devote only a few pages to each.

Fig. 17.6.

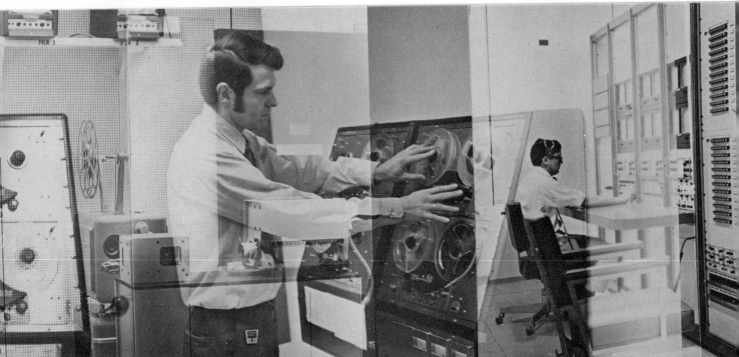

18. Print Reproduction

THE COMMERCIAL ARTIST cannot very well divorce himself from a knowledge of the methods by which his artwork is reproduced. This is true for two reasons: a knowledge of reproduction methods will enable him to prepare his work so that it will produce the desired effect on the printed page; furthermore, his artwork must be prepared to conform with the mechanical requirements or restrictions of the reproduction process employed, the kind of paper to be used, etc.

Production procedures is a vast subject that can only be touched upon here. A visit to a photoengraver's shop, newspaper, commercial printing or lithography plant is highly recommended. Many of the larger ones conduct plant tours for students and graphic arts groups, and you are apt to learn far more on one of these visits than from reams of literature on the subject. Telephone or write to such establishments requesting permission to join the next scheduled plant tour. Another source of visual information on these processes is films and slides—some available on loan free of charge from printing associations and photo materials manufacturers.

Letterpress, Lithography and Gravure

There are three major print methods of reproducing art and copy: by letterpress, offset lithography and gravure. Each has its advantages and disadvantages. Occasionally a publication may have some pages prepared by one method and the rest by another, depending upon the nature of the material, the effect desired and the number of copies printed. When artwork is to be reproduced by these standard printing processes, it is first photocopied on film, in the same size in which it is to be printed, and this film is used to make a photographic image of the original on the printing plate. For letterpress, this image is in relief on the plate (*Fig. 18.1*); in lithography, it is level with the surface (*Fig. 18.2*); and in rotogravure, it is etched or incised on a metal cylinder (*Fig. 18.3*). In letterpress printing, the ink (indicated in blue) is on the *raised* surface of the plate; in lithography, it is on the *flat* surface; and in gravure, it is in the etched or *recessed* areas.

Fig. 18.1: Relief Printing—Letterpress.

Fig. 18.2: Planographic Printing—Lithography.

Fig. 18.3: Intaglio Printing—Gravure.

BASIC STAGES OF PHOTO OFFSET PRINTING.

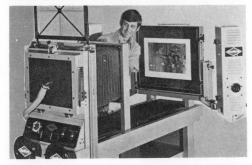

Fig. 18.4: Art and/or Type Proofs Photocopied on Film.

Fig. 18.4 A: Negatives Positioned on Flat.

Fig. 18.5: Negatives on Flat Exposed to Plate.

Fig. 18.6: Offset Plate Is Developed.

Denton Publications   Fig. 18.7: Plate Put on Press and Printed.

Offset lithography is now the most extensively used printing process. In this process, the artwork or type proofs are photocopied on film (*Fig. 18.4*). The resulting assemblage of negatives (*Fig. 18.4A*) is exposed to a sensitized offset plate (*Fig. 18.5*), which is developed (*Fig. 18.6*) and then placed on the printing press (*Fig. 18.7*), inked and printed. For black-and-white or one-color printing, only one plate is necessary to reproduce the image, but for two or more colors a different plate is used for each color, and the paper or cloth being printed has to be run through the press for each color if a single-color press is used. There are also presses capable of printing two, three or four colors in successive register; on such presses each sheet of paper passes through the press only once.

Full-Color Processes

Where full-color halftone reproduction is required—that is, a complete range of colors, with shadings and blending of color and tone involved—three- or four-color printing is used, with one plate for each of the primary colors. Here, use is made of the fact that red (magenta), yellow and blue (cyan) can be mixed to make any other color, theoretically at least. These colors are not actually mixed, but are printed as tiny dots over or alongside each other on the paper to produce, optically, the appearance of many colors. Black is added as a separate plate in four-color printing to produce better definition.

In very accurate reproductions, it may be necessary to use up to a dozen or more different colors, where, for instance, two or three different reds or other colors are required which cannot be closely matched by the four-color method. At times it is necessary to use solid colors, as in packaging and textiles, and each color is printed from a separate plate or roller.

The photographic and mechanical processes, as well as changes in materials (inks, paper stock) and in size from original to reproduced art are all factors in making the reproduction differ, sometimes drastically, from the original.

Line and Continuous Tone Art Reproduction

As briefly explained in Chapter 2, with regard to reproduction, all artwork, for both print and nonprint media, whether in color or "black and white," fits into either of two categories—*line* art (*Fig. 18.8*) or *continuous tone* art (*Fig. 18.9*) —or a combination of both (*Fig. 18.10*). (We use the term "art" rather broadly to mean any graphic material, whether it be a drawing, painting, photograph, lettering, type, shading sheet, film overlay, etc.)

The same terms and principles apply to color art. If the color is solid, not gradations or variations of the color, it is line art. If there are gradations, even in only one hue, such as red, it is continuous tone art.

When imaging line art on a plate for printing, it is first photocopied *directly* as a film negative (or positive in some processes), and the printing plate is made from this film image. Unfortunately, the major printing processes in use at present are not capable of registering continuous tone images on a printing plate; therefore continuous tone art must first be photocopied through a "screen" which converts the various tones to solid black and white dots or patterns of various sizes that give the appearance of tonal gradations to the naked eye. This is known as a "halftone" image, or a halftone plate, when it reaches the plate stage. *Figs. 18.13-18.14* help to clarify this.

The traditional screen consists of two sheets of glass sandwiched together. More recently, the *film* halftone screen has been introduced. It consists of a durable transparent substance, such as mylar film, with the screen image pattern photographically imaged on it, either in magenta color or gray. The magenta color allows for the use of filters to manipulate contrast in the image pattern; the gray screens are generally used for color platemaking. Film screens are less expensive and easier to handle than glass screens. All screens are available in various sheet sizes and dot sizes. For coarse reproduction, such as in newspapers, a screen with 65 lines per inch is used; for magazine reproduction on coated paper stock a screen of 120 or more lines may be used. The finer the screen and the smoother the paper stock on which it is printed, the better the reproduction—that is, the more faithfully it will reproduce the detail and tone values of the original art or photography.

Fig. 18.8: Line Art.   Anna Marie Magagna

Fig. 18.9 A: Continuous Tone Art.

Fig. 18.9B: Halftone   Enlarged Section.

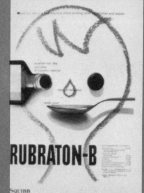
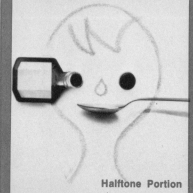

RUBRATON-B

Halftone Portion

Milton Herder

114

Fig. 18.10: Combination Line and Halftone Art.

Fig. 18.11: Glass Screen Pattern.

Fig. 18.12: Magenta Screen Pattern.

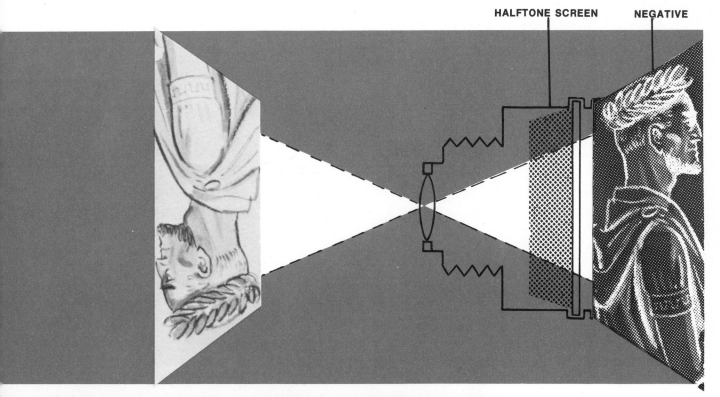

HALFTONE SCREEN   NEGATIVE

Fig. 18.13: Art Being Photo-copied Through Halftone Screen.

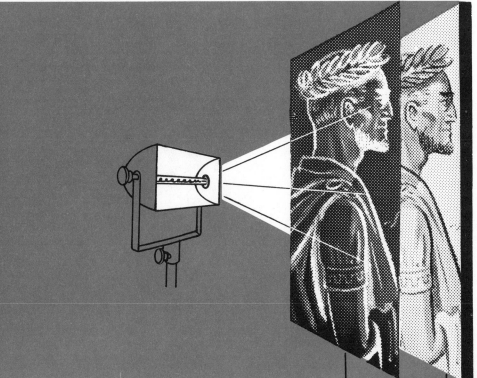

Fig. 18.14: Positive Print (Velox) or Offset Plate Made from Halftone Negative (After Exposure and Development).

HALFTONE NEGATIVE – SCREENED   POSITIVE PRINT

Veloxes

When a copy negative is made of continuous tone art or photographs for platemaking, the negative image consists of the screened dot pattern necessary for halftone printing. If this halftone negative is used to make a contact print on paper, the resulting positive image will also be made up of the dot pattern contained in the negative. This print is known as a *screened velox*. Technically, the screened velox is now line copy, having been converted to only black-and-white images; therefore it can be pasted in page or layout position with other line copy, such as line drawings, logotypes, etc., and the entire assemblage recopied as a line negative. The printing plate, letterpress or offset, can now be made from this negative.

There are several advantages to this method of using veloxes: it is less expensive than making a combination line and halftone plate; it is more convenient and easier to assemble the varied copy units in print form than in film negative form for platemaking; additions, corrections and changes can be made more readily in the print paste-up stage; the client and layout artist can judge the effect or appearance better in the positive image stage. This procedure is more applicable to medium and coarse halftone screens, up to a 120-line screen, than for finer halftones.

Fig. 18.16: A "Square Halftone" Retains the Screen Pattern in Both the Solid White and Solid Black Areas of the Original.

Fig. 18.17: The Highlight or Dropout Halftone Has Solid White Areas

Fig. 18.18: The Combination Line and Dropout Has Both Solid Whites and Blacks.

Fig. 18.19: 85 Line Screen Halftone

Fig. 18.20: 65 Line Screen Halftone

Photo by Beki Maurello

VALLEY NEWS

Elizabethtown, N.Y.

Richard Roberts Named National Bureau of Standards

President Richard M. Nixon announced Dec. 20 the nomination of Dr. Richard W. Roberts as Director of the National Bureau of Standards.

Dr. Roberts is currently manager of Materials Science and Engineering at the General Electric Research and Development Center in Schenectady.

In his new post, the 37-year-old GE scientist will direct the activities of the National Bureau of Standards, which is responsible for maintaining and developing national standards of measurement. In addition, the NBS conducts extensive studies in many fields, including materials, applications of technology, computer sciences and technology, consumer protection standards, building research, and standards for health and safety, law enforcement, and environmental control (including noise control and air and water pollution standards).

At the GE Research and Development Center, Dr. Roberts directs the activities of a staff of more than 250 scientists and engineers who have produced numerous advances in many different areas of technology. Major breakthroughs include the first gem-quality diamonds to be produced in the laboratory, significant advances in coal gasification research, unique cutting tools for machining space-age metals and alloys, new composite materials, a pollution free coating technique, a revolutionary solid waste recycling process using special strains of bacteria, a wide variety of medical sensors and diagnostic devices, and the world's most powerful permanent magnets.

A native of Buffalo, Dr. Roberts received his bachelor's degree with distinction in 1956 from the University of Rochester and his doctorate in physical chemistry in 1959 from Brown University. After serving as a National Academy of Science Postdoctoral Fellow at the National Bureau of Standards, he joined the staff of the General Electric Research Laboratory (now part of the Research and Development Center) in 1960.

As a research scientist, Dr. Roberts gained international recognition for his studies of ultrahigh vacuum technology, the physical and chemical properties of automatically clean metal and semiconductor surfaces, chemical kinetics, and the lubrication of space-age metals. Among other achievements, he played a major role in the development of a new family of lubricants that make it possible to use titanium.

Becky Maurello, local artist whose work will be on display at the Social Center, January 7 and 14

Social Center Plans Crafts Open House

The Elizabethtown Social Center will host a crafts open house on two consecutive Sundays, January 7 and 14, from 3 to 6 p.m. Artists will demonstrate weaving, spinning, rug making, photography, pottery, knitting, fly tying, leathercraft, and drawing. Anyone interested in learning these skills can then sign up for a six-week class beginning the week of January 15. The demonstrations are free and all are welcome to attend. Materials fees for the six-week classes run from ten to twenty dollars.

Crafts will be demonstrated by local artists, including Becky Maurello (pottery), Lacy Schiess (leathercraft), Tibbins Gross (spinning and weaving), John Hatt (fly tying), Sarah Swan (hooked rugs), Rosemarie Christian (knitting), and John Cullen (drawing techniques). These same artists will offer instruction in the six-week classes.

The open houses are part of an effort to revive an extensive craft program at the Center. Courses in leathercraft, spinning, and weaving were initiated last November and attracted interest from both children and adults. A new darkroom is currently under construction at the Center, and if enough interest is shown the pottery kiln and workshop will be renovated and reopened.

The community crafts program centers around informal craft groups open to both children and adults. Materials fees are kept to a minimum, with most of the equipment supplied by the Center. Emphasis is on beginning skills, although there is opportunity for advanced instruction and practice. Most classes will be run through the winter, with facilities for individual work open all year. If enough interest is shown, summer courses will be offered. Beyond the personal satisfaction of learning a craft, it is hoped that the program will provide incentive for the development of local craft industries.

Friday Night To Feature Adirondack Life

Winter activity begins this Friday, January 5, at the Adirondack Center Museum in Elizabethtown with the first of a winter-long series of "Friday Nights at the Museum."

This first program will be the brief but spectacular history of Adirondack Life, the popular quarterly published in Willsboro. Mr. Lionel Atwill, editor, will discuss the past, present, and future of the magazine, illustrating his remarks with samples of staff photography that has helped make circulation soar in four short years.

The Museum will open at 7 p.m. this Friday, and the program will begin at 8 p.m. A social hour with refreshments will follow the presentation at which time visitors may talk with the speaker or browse through the museum's bookstore.

Sponsored by the Essex County Historical Society, these Friday night programs are open to everyone. There is no admission charge. Membership in the Society, likewise, is open to all. Essex County residents or not.

The complete schedule of programs will be available Friday and will be publicized thruout the north country next week.

Essex Co. Economy Growing Faster

Special to Valley News

Just how much the Essex County economy has moved forward in the last few years, despite the nation's domestic problems, may be gathered from a look at the record books.

They show that the volume of retail business done in the local area, a principal indicator of the state of the economy, rose significantly in the five years ending January 1, 1972.

The gain was made in the face of general apprehension about unemployment, crime conditions, racial strife, swelling welfare rolls, inflation, the war and higher taxes.

The progress made in the local area in the period is revealed in figures compiled by the Standard Rate and Data Service.

They show that retail sales in Essex County stores, as of the beginning of this year, reached an annual rate of over $65,687,000. Five years previously they totalled $50,131,000.

This was equivalent to consumer spending at the rate of $6,105 per local household, as compared with the 1966 rate of $4,672 per household.

The rise was greater than that recorded in many parts of the country. It amounted to 31 percent. Elsewhere in the United States, it was 21 percent. In the Middle Atlantic States, it was 28 percent.

Fundamental to the growth in retail activity in the local area during the five-year span was the marked increase in real income achieved by most families.

It has been on an upward curve, more than compensating for the rising cost of living due to tax hikes, bigger grocery and rent bills and zooming medical costs.

Nationally, according to the Bureau of Labor Statistics, the cost of living has gone up 33 percent since 1965, but weekly wages have climbed by 44 percent.

Figures for Essex County show that personal income in the area, after deduction for taxes, went from $81,807,000 to $111,739,000 in the five years.

With more money at their command, consumers are spending more freely now than they have for some time. They are, by the same token, saving less.

As a result, merchants are ringing up record sales. The big pickup has been in automobiles, furniture, appliances, floor coverings and other durable goods.

Training for Junior Bobsled Drivers Set

After the very successful junior bobsled races at Mt. Van Hoevenberg Dec. 27, Dr. Robert Lopez and his Kiwanis Club committee met with Mrs. Alice Beeckel and bobrun superintendent Joe McKillip about training junior drivers. As a result of that conversation, beginning Jan. 2, daily from 2 to 4 p.m., junior bobsledders will be able to train on the run. Age 14 to 18 can slide and licenses to drive will be given to boys or girls age 16 and up. There will be a $5 registration fee and no other charge for sliding. Youngsters age 14 to 18 can register by telephoning 523-3111.

Fig. 18.21: A Page Assembly of Halftone Veloxes and Type Proofs which Can Now Be Copied as Line Negative. Courtesy of Denton Publications   Selected Portion Enlarged.

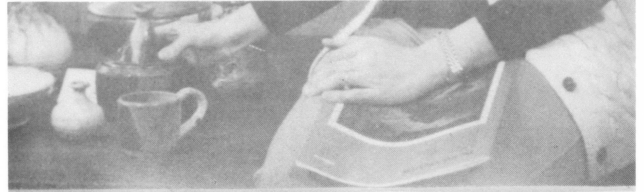

...tist whose work will be on display at the   Social Center, January 7 and 14

...nter Plans Crafts Open Hou

Social   Swan (hooked rugs), Rosemarie
s open   Christian (knitting), and John   fees are kept to a minimum, most of the equipment supp

Fig. 19.1: A Multiple Screen Lecture Hall in Use. State University of New York, Plattsburgh.   Photo by John Lonergan.

19. Nonprint Reproduction

IN ADDITION to the usual print media—books, instruction sheets, manuals, charts, etc.— schools and other educational institutions and programs utilize many graphic, *nonprint* forms of communication and instruction. Most visual nonprint teaching methods involve a film pro- jection system utilizing various kinds and sizes of film for the verbal and visual message carrier. Projectors and screens vary in form and size, depending upon the system. Projec- tion systems in popular use are slide, overhead transparency, filmstrip, microfilm and microfiche. Other popular nonprint media are television, computer assisted instruction systems and various "learning machines." Of course, audio systems—tape, record or live voice—can be used in conjunction with these.

Fig. 19.2: Television in the Classroom.

Fig. 19.4: Self Instruction, Slide-Sound Rear Projection System.

Fig. 19.3: Instructor Using Overhead Projection System. State University of New York, Plattsburgh.

Nonprint media are used not only in schools, but also for sales conferences, in-service training, museum programs, displays, etc. Art preparation, production methods and requirements for some of these systems will be briefly presented in this chapter.

The equipment used for mediated instruction is known as the *hardware,* whereas the actual instructional material or program is known as the *software.* For example, television cameras, control consoles, tape recording units, etc. are hardware; but the lesson plan, the tape on which the program or lesson is recorded is the software. A motion picture *film* is software; the *projector* is hardware. The graphic artist is involved with preparing software, but, as in production procedures for print materials, he must have some understanding of the methods and requirements of the system used—perhaps even more so for nonprint materials because each nonprint system has rigid formats and restrictions.

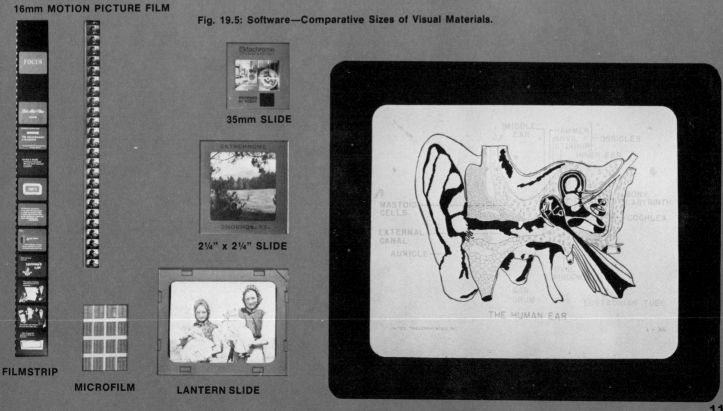

Fig. 19.5: Software—Comparative Sizes of Visual Materials.

16mm MOTION PICTURE FILM

FOCUS

35mm SLIDE

2¼" x 2¼" SLIDE

FILMSTRIP

MICROFILM

LANTERN SLIDE

OVERHEAD TRANSPARENCY

119

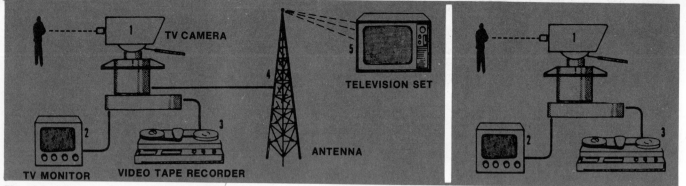

Fig. 19.6: Schematic of Broadcast Television Systems.

Closed Circuit Television Systems.

Television Art

The television medium, broadcasting countless commercials, credits, entertainment and instructional programs day and night from hundreds of stations, has a voracious appetite for artwork, both typographic and illustrative in black and white and color. Designers, artists, and photographers are used by television stations, networks and related services to produce the commercials, both still and animated, as well as the visuals, captions and credit lines, the cartoons, the sets and props, etc.

There is not much difference between public broadcasting and commercial broadcasting insofar as the artist is concerned, except for program content, operational funds and size of staff. There are two types of television transmission systems: *broadcast* television transmits its signals through the atmosphere via antennae from station to station, or station to individual TV receivers (*Fig. 19.6*); *closed circuit* television, on the other hand, transmits its signals via cables from the studio control room to the receivers, and they can thus be picked up only by receivers linked directly to those cables—a limited range. Closed circuit TV is used for instructional, communications, informational and security purposes in a building or group of near-by buildings, such as on a college campus. Many public broadcasting stations of the Channel 13 type are known as educational stations and may even be part of a network. Television serving a solely instructional purpose may be closed circuit, as in an individual school, or can be broadcast, as in a school district serving several district schools.

Television may be "live," in which case the program or activity is transmitted directly from the TV cameras as it is being performed, or it may be "taped," with the picture and sound recorded electronically on tape and played or transmitted at some later time. Television can be taped at the same time it is being transmitted "live." In addition, a disclike unit can record portions of the activity, to provide immediate on-the-spot playbacks, as in sports telecasts.

One of the many advantages of television is this ability of the image to be transmitted immediately or put on tape and played back immediately for viewing, without having to wait hours or days for processing, as in cinematography. Also, since it can be recorded and played back one section at a time, it can be erased from the tape, and any minute or lengthy section immediately wiped off the tape and re-recorded or re-shot, then and there. A person can be recorded while speaking, and later visuals can be dubbed in, eliminating the person's image from particular portions without disturbing the speaker's voice.

Preparing Visuals for TV

The graphics materials prepared for TV are known as "visuals." They may be used directly "on camera" (*Fig. 19.7*) up through a film chain, a multiple component device which, on signal from the director of the control board, projects a 35mm slide or a motion picture film into the TV circuit via a small stationary camera that is part of the film chain (*Fig. 19.8*). It is also possi-

Fig. 19.7: TV Visual Shown "on Camera".

Fig. 19.8: The Film Chain.

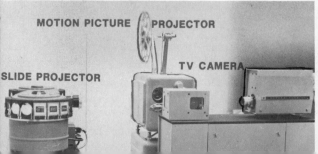

Fig. 19.9: Set-up for Projected Television Visual.

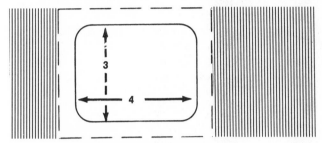

Fig. 19.10: Format for TV Visual.

Fig. 19.11: Fine Detail and Small Lettering Cannot Be Seen.

ble to pick up a visual on camera from a 35 mm or 3½" x 4" slide projected *(Fig. 19.9)* onto a screen in the studio, as is done in news broadcasts, where the visual and the announcer can be seen simultaneously. Slide projection can be made from the front or the rear of the screen, depending upon the situation and the type of screen used. Overhead projectuals can also be projected front or rear screen and picked up by the camera. For direct pickup by the camera, visuals are usually prepared as various forms of "camera cards" (pages 41 and 85).

The mechanical requirements for TV visuals are definite: *proportionally,* the visuals must be made in a 3 to 4 ratio and in *horizontal* format, to conform to the TV screen *(Fig. 19.10)*. The TV screen is not capable of fine *resolution*; therefore, artwork has to be definite in tone, color and line. Subtle variations and fine detail are lost in transmission. A broad *contrast* range from pure black to pure white in the same visual presents problems; therefore a narrower value range is used (Fig. 19.9-19.11). The *area* of the visual picked up by the camera may vary somewhat from the image transmitted by the receiver, so important material must not be too close to the edges of the visual, especially the corners.

Camera cards for television are drawn on gray or colored stock, usually bristol or illustration board that is stiff enough to be self-supporting on an easel. A 9-inch high x 12-inch wide image with a 3-inch clear border all around makes a good working and storage size. For something larger, like a weather map, where one needs to show only portions at a time as well as the overall view, one could go to 3 feet x 4 feet or more. A zoom lens on the camera enables the cameraman to enlarge a selected portion of the image and show it full screen size on the TV receiver.

Titles and names are often superimposed over an image or person. This is done by making the title on a separate card or slide, with white letters on a black background. Title and person are combined either by means of two cameras—one on the person and another on the "super"—or by picking up the super from a slide in the film chain, thus requiring only one camera. When the title or second image electronically "cuts out" the background image it replaces, it is known as "keying in." Much animation is used in television; this is done by cinematography, and either incorporated in the live program or on tape, through the film chain.

The "Super" Card

Fig. 19.12: Title or Name Can Be "Supered" on Subject.

Television Commercials—
Storyboards

A large and important proportion of visual advertising, both local and national, utilizes the medium of television. Because television transmits a moving image, as well as typographic message, plus voice and sound, it differs drastically from print advertising, with regard to design and production.

Local commercials are generally prepared as color slides, TV cards and photographs; but regional and national commercials are usually made as 16mm color motion pictures, though some are done as 35mm films, with synchronized sound. Because of the enormous cost of network television time, as well as the cost of producing the television commercials, much consideration, planning and evaluation are involved before a commercial is actually made.

The client whose service or product is to be advertised consults with the "account executive" of the advertising agency which handles that particular account. Within the advertising agency the account executive works with the copywriter who, perhaps in conjunction with a "creative director," will conceive ideas for a commercial, or series of them. This must be visualized for the client by means of a storyboard consisting of artwork and script, generally in rough form at first. The roughs will be followed by a more finished storyboard of about eight frames, which will establish settings, characters, dress, props, mood, picture angles, etc. This, along with written production information, will be used to elicit bids from television production studios when the commercial has been finally decided upon by the client and advertising agency. If a set is to be built, the production studio will submit a sketch for approval before construction. Talent (actors/performers) will be selected, a wardrobe obtained or made, props secured, etc. About 7 weeks are required from date of granting the bid to date of finished production. The commercial will generally be made on film or video tape. The film will be edited, a work print made and then copy prints obtained for distribution to the television networks or stations.

Fig. 19.13A: Finished Drawing for a Storyboard Frame. Nick LaMicela, Norman Craig & Kummel, Inc.

(See Fig. 19.15 for a complete storyboard.)

Fig. 19.13B: A Photo Storyboard.

Fig. 19.14: Design of Set to Be Used to Film a TV Commercial. Georg James, Designer.

1.

ECU OF GIRL'S HAND WITH
WRITING LETTER. TELESCOPE
NTER NEARBY.

IC: ROMANTIC VIOLIN ARRANGE-
OF OLD SPICE SONG IN
STMAS MANNER)

(V.O.): My Dearest Phillip,
hristmas is upon us once again

2.

ROMANTIC SCENE OF BEAUTIFUL GIRL
AT EXPENSIVE DESK IN ELEGANT ROOM
WRITING HER "ONE AND ONLY". SNOW
IS FALLING OUTSIDE. SHE IS IN
ROBE. THERE IS A DEMI-TASSE.

what better symbol of our sensitive
and deep relation

3.

WE CONTINUE TO ROMANCE SCENE, AS
THE COMMERICAL PROGRESSES. THERE
ARE A VARIETY OF OLD SPICE GIFT
SETS AND DECANTERS ON THE DESK.

than this Old Spice telescope
decanter.

4.

CON'T ACTION

Because in my mind's eye though
continents may stand between us, I
see only you.

5.

6.

SHE FOLDS LETTER AND ATTACHES

SHE PICKS ANOTHER DECANTER FROM
LARGE SELECTION ON DESK. (SUPER:

8.

SHE BEGINS ANOTHER LETTER TO

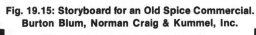

**Fig. 19.15: Storyboard for an Old Spice Commercial.
Burton Blum, Norman Craig & Kummel, Inc.**

(Several frames from the actual film
clip are shown for comparison.)

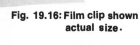

**Fig. 19.16: Film clip shown
actual size.**

Fig. 19.17: An Overhead Projector.

Fig. 19.18: Set-up for Overhead Projection. Courtesy of Technifax Education Division.

Overhead Transparencies

The overhead transparency, used in conjunction with the overhead projector (*Fig. 19.17*), provides a very useful and popular media system. It enables the instructor or speaker to face the class or audience (*Fig. 19.18*), to project in a lighted room, to present prepared material at any desired pace, to return to or retain the image as desired and, if necessary, to present material as it is being written, drawn or diagrammed during presentation to the audience. In addition, a prepared visual can be projected and further images superimposed in stages by merely placing additional transparencies over the previous ones (*Figs. 19.19-19.20*), or a single visual can be revealed in stages. Commercially prepared transparencies are available; but often the instructor, students or professional staff of the school or institution using them prefer to prepare their own. An "overhead" is large enough for art to

be prepared at the same size at which it will be used. It can be used with or without a frame or mount, though a frame is useful for handling and is especially necessary if overlays are used. From a key drawing or drawings as many transparencies as necessary can easily and economically be produced.

DESIGN AND PRODUCTION

On the next page is shown the procedure for drawing and making an overhead transparency. The objective of this particular visual is to show the direct airline route from Tokyo to Moscow. It is planned for three-stage use: (1) a base transparency in black showing ⌐ ··· and identifying names; (2) an overlay in blue showing land mass areas; and (3) the "direct line route" shown as a heavy dotted line. The finished transparencies are shown below (*Figs. 19.19-19.20*).

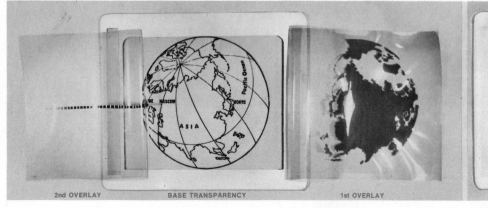

2nd OVERLAY   BASE TRANSPARENCY   1st OVERLAY

Fig. 19.19: Overhead Projectual with Overlays.

Fig. 19.20: Overlays in Position.

Fig. 19.21.   **Fig. 19.22.**   **Fig. 19.23.**

PROCEDURE

A world globe is used as reference for the drawing (*Fig. 19.21*).

An ink outline is drawn on thin bristol board at the same size as the planned transparency image (*Fig. 19.22.*).

Location names are done with transfer lettering directly on the drawing (*Fig. 19.23*).

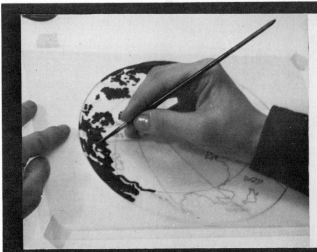

Fig. 19.24.   **Fig. 19.25.**

Tracing paper is placed over the world drawing, and the land areas are drawn in solid black with a brush and India ink (*Figs. 19.24-19.25*). A light table or light box (sheet of frosted glass with a light beneath it) is helpful for seeing the underlying drawing through the tracing paper.

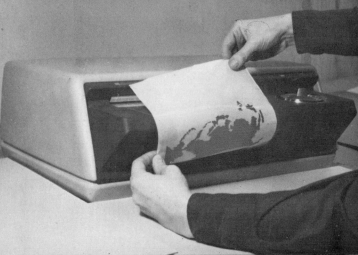

Fig. 19.26.   **Fig. 19.27.**   **Fig. 19.28.**

A sheet of blue imaging Thermofax transparency film is placed over the land drawing (*Fig. 19.26*).

The imaging sheet and drawing are inserted in the upper slot of the Thermofax Copier, issuing from the bottom slot seconds later with a blue image (*Figs. 19.27-19.28*). The black outline drawing is processed in the same way using black imaging film. A section of transparent dotted line tape (page 64) is applied in position on a sheet of clear acetate for the third overlay, showing the direct line route (*Fig. 19.20*).

125

20. Careers in Commercial Art

MANY AVENUES of employment are open to the commercial artist. The beginner, just out of school and with no practical working experience in the field, has the biggest problem. "Everyone wants experienced artists," the beginner wails. "How about all the training I've had in art school, doesn't it count?" Of course it counts, just as the neophyte physician's eight years of medical studies count—but they do not qualify him to jump from the classroom to the operating room to perform a major brain operation.

Even four years of art school training are just a foundation for the commercial artist. Of course, a lot depends upon one's initial qualifications and objectives. Several students undertaking the same training from the same instructor will produce work of varying quality. Some students learn more rapidly than others, some do very well in a particular phase of commercial art, but seem unsuited for any other. One of the functions of a school is to guide as well as train the student.

I find that the student is likely to do best what he is most interested in, both from the point of view of subject matter and the selection of a specific field such as layout, fashion illustration, textile design, etc. The illustrator may not enjoy the study of perspective or anatomy, but will find them necessary to accomplish his objectives. Too many students want to get to work before they are actually ready for it. Your employer will be paying you to produce, not to learn on the job; and while any organization employing a beginner realizes that a certain amount of learning will have to take place, it also realizes that the better trained you are to begin with, the more dependable and useful you will be.

Good places to start work are in art departments of *small* studios, advertising agencies, publications, television studios, or as an assistant to a competent free-lance artist. Here you will be closer to the actual artwork, and while it may not sound as impressive as a big name agency, you are not so likely to be pigeon-holed for several years. If you cannot progress very far in your first place of employment, the experience will stand you in good stead and make you more useful to the larger organizations.

Until you have had considerable experience it is not advisable to freelance, and then it is best to have one or two dependable accounts before making a decisive break from your job. Freelancing requires business competence as well as art ability and often entails a broader scope of work than a salaried position. Cost estimates on jobs have to be given in advance. Not only the work to be done, but for whom and the use to which it will be put have to be taken into consideration when pricing. Too high an estimate may mean the loss of an assignment, too low an estimate may mean monetary loss to you. Aside from any consideration of reputation or other factors, a safe method is to determine the amount of time the work will require and price it on a total fee based on an hourly rate, plus allowance for overhead, materials, consultation with the client, necessary research, etc. For certain assignments of a repetitive nature—for example, book jackets of a particular line of books, textile designs or greeting cards, the manufacturer, studio or publisher will have standard prices. In such cases you can adjust your work to the price; or seek a line of better quality, paying higher prices.

Fig. 20.1: Looseleaf Display Portfolio Joshua Meier Co., Inc.

Reference File

A reference, or "swipe" file, is indispensable to any commercial artist. This may be made up of a continuously expanding collection of printed or photographic material of value to the artist, either as a source of factual information or to stimulate ideas for a design or illustration. While it is not ethical to copy another person's work, it is practical and often necessary to use such material as a springboard for one's own imagination, and for visual information where accuracy of setting or subject matter is required. There are very few highly original things in this world . . . most of them have their origin in some previous work!

Interesting layouts or compositions, lettering samples, texture representations, color schemes, abstract designs rendering techniques, old engravings, well designed packages and anything else of general or specific relationship to your particular domain of the commercial art field should be clipped and filed. Such subject matter as architectural material, sports activities, action figures, facial expressions, hands, etc. are of importance to the illustrator and designer.

Newspapers, magazines, direct mail pieces and even your own snapshots are sources for this file. As you peruse a magazine for clippings, select the pages desired and write the subject heading in the upper right hand corner before cutting. These pages can be filed in legal sized envelopes with appropriate titles. It is best to remove the flap from the envelope and slit one side open for easier access to the envelope. Keep the envelopes, arranged vertically rather than flat, in a kraftboard file case, or a metal filing cabinet of legal size. Each envelope should have a tab in the upper right hand corner identifying the subject matter. The material can be listed under such general headings as Animals, Transportation, etc., or, if the collection is large a more detailed breakdown used, such as Animals, horses; Animals, dogs; Animals, cats, etc.

Since clipping and filing are tedious jobs, and human beings, especially artists, tend to procrastinate where tediousness is involved, it is advisable to do a certain amount of this once or twice a week so as not to crowd yourself out of house and studio with an incendiary collection of old newspapers and magazines. Five or six folders may serve as temporary storage for a general breakdown while clipping the material, and then once every three or four weeks the final filing can be done. If you do not do your own clipping and filing it is best to run through the material occasionally, not only to familiarize yourself with it, but also to check on the manner in which it is being filed, especially if the person doing it does not also do artwork.

GLOSSARY

Account Executive—member of an advertising agency who handles a client's advertising, serving as liaison man between client and agency.

Bleed—to trim into the printed matter of a page, as on pages 20 and 22 of this book. Artwork must be prepared about a quarter of an inch beyond the outside edges of the page.

Body Type—the type commonly used for reading matter, as distinguished from DISPLAY TYPE, which is used for headlines.

Caps—abbreviation for capital letters, as distinguished from lower case, or small letters.

Caption—heading of a chapter, section or page. Also the descriptive matter under or accompanying an illustration.

Center Spread—space occupied by an advertisement on the two facing center pages of a publication—actually a continuous sheet.

Character—in computing type, any single unit such as a letter, punctuation mark or word space.

Column—vertical divisions of a page.

Column Depth—dimension of a column space, measured from the top of the page to the bottom. A column inch would be a section of the column one inch deep, and the full width of the column.

Continuous Tone—any graphic material which contains gradient tones, either from black to white or from solid colors to tints.

Copy—reading matter or text as distinguished from illustrative material. Sometimes used to cover both.

Copy Writer—person who writes the text of an ad or brochure.

Cropping—marking off the desired area or section of a photograph or artwork. The marks used to designate the boundaries are called "crop marks."

Direct Mail Advertising—any advertising material in the form of a single sheet, folded sheet, booklet, postcard, etc., made up for mailing directly to the prospective buyer.

Display Art—placards, posters, or racks used to display merchandise in store windows, on counters, and other appropriate places.

Double Page Spread—the space occupied by two facing sheets in a magazine or newspaper. Called a CENTER SPREAD when it is in the center of the magazine.

Dummy—a preliminary visualization of a booklet or other printed or display material, usually folded, cut-out or made three-dimensional, to the exact size of the proposed work.

Flat Tone—a tone which is uniform in value throughout the area it encompasses, as distinguished from a "graded tone."

Font—complete assortment of all the different characters of one particular style and size of type.

Format—the size, shape, style, etc., of a publication.

Free-Lance Artist—one who works independently, and on a fee basis, rather than on salary for only one company.

Graded Tone—a tone which varies from light to dark, as compared with a flat tone, which is uniform in value.

Halftone—the transformation of continuous tone art or copy into dots of varying sizes by photographing it through a glass or plastic crossline screen.

Highlight—the lightest areas of a painting or drawing, usually small, crisp, white accents.

Layout—the arrangement and form given to the various units of illustrative and reading material on any form of printed matter.

Leading—the insertion of metal strips between lines of letterpress type to increase the space between them. The spaces between lines can thus be increased as desired. Without leading the lines are said to be "set solid."

Media—the vehicle through which the advertisement is presented. This may be a newspaper, magazine, direct mail, radio, tv, etc. Also, the working materials, such as pen and ink, water-color, etc.

Overlay—a sheet of transparent paper or acetate placed over artwork to indicate where additional artwork color, or lettering is to appear.

Photostat—or "Stat." A photographic reproduction made from a paper negative instead of a film negative. A stat can be either a positive or a negative, and this should be indicated when ordering.

Point-Of-Sale Advertising—promotion method used in stores where the product is sold. This usually is done with display cards, streamers, display cartons and similar media.

Positive—a photographic image on paper, glass or film which corresponds to the original insofar as values are concerned. A reversal of values would result in a negative image.

Process Plates—photoengraving plates for printing two, three or four colors, one over the other, to produce a final desired effect.

Production Manager—the man in an advertising agency or publishing house who is responsible for processing the hundred or more separate production jobs required, from idea to finished ad or book. It is his job to supervise and "follow up" the progress of all the work from copy through layout, art, client okay, engraving, typesetting, electrotyping, printing, folding and binding operations, etc. It is in his department that many young assistants learn the fundamentals of graphic arts procedures.

Proof—an inked impression of composed type or a plate, taken for the purpose of inspecting or pasting up with other lettering or artwork.

Register—accurate correspondence of type and art elements in printing or preparation of artwork. In color printing, register means correct superimposition of each plate so that the color of each plate falls exactly where it should in relation to the others.

Scaling—the process of determining the exact size of artwork or photographs for reduction or enlargement.

Screen—a cross-ruled sheet of glass or plastic which is placed between the film and lens of a camera when copying artwork or photography for reproduction. This breaks up the copy into the various sizes of dots, from the lightest grays to almost solid blacks, that form a halftone.

Spot—a small drawing, usually used as a decoration or an accessory to the major illustration.

Surprint—a photoengraving in which a line-plate effect appears over the face of a halftone, or vice versa. Also, to print over the face of material which has already been printed.

Trade Mark—any device which identifies the origin of a product, or the organization which makes it. It can be a symbol or a name, or both.

Vignette—a halftone in which the edges fade off gradually to a light gray or white. In some instances only part of the halftone may be finished in vignette.